Northwest Vista College
Learning Resource Center
3535 North Ellison Drive
San Antonio, Texas 78251

Things That Go Bump
volume 1

Things That Go Bump

Volume 1, Plays for Young Adults

edited by Kit Brennan

Cover design by Doowah Design.
This book was printed on Ancient Forest Friendly paper.
Printed and bound in Canada by Marquis Book Printing Inc.

We acknowledge the support of the Canada Council for the Arts and the Manitoba Arts Council for our publishing program.

Library and Archives Canada Cataloguing in Publication

Things that go bump / Kit Brennan, editor.

ISBN 978-1-897109-36-6 (v. 1)

1. Young adult drama, Canadian (English).
2. Canadian drama (English)--21st century.
I. Brennan, Kit, 1957-

PS8307.T55 2009   jC812'.60809283   C2009-906526-6

Signature Editions
P.O. Box 206, RPO Corydon, Winnipeg, Manitoba, R3M 3S7
www.signature-editions.com

Contents

Foreword

This volume contains five recent Canadian plays for young adult audiences. Three of the plays were originally written for touring to secondary schools (*In This World, Offensive Fouls* and *To Be Frank*). *Learning the Game* has toured via the Fringe and community groups as well as in schools. *Binti's Journey* is designed for the interesting senior-elementary/junior-high age group (Grades 7 to 9, give or take a year either way); it is an adaptation for the theatre of Deborah Ellis' novel for young people, *The Heaven Shop*.

These plays are about real and current issues for young adults, written by writers who are involved and connected with this demographic for reasons of their own which also are varied and individual. The plays were commissioned or assisted by some of Canada's foremost companies in the field of Theatre for Young Audiences — Geordie Theatre and Youtheatre, both in Montreal, Theatre Direct in Toronto, Manitoba Theatre for Young People in Winnipeg, Concrete Theatre in Edmonton, and All Nations Theatre in Calgary. Also involved along the way were provincial Arts Councils, playwrights' and writers' centres, universities and theatre schools, individual dramaturges, artistic directors, and fellow writers and artists.

The playwrights have a wealth of theatrical and life experience: Hannah Moscovitch is currently playwright-in-residence at Toronto's Tarragon Theatre; Jason Long teaches writing for adults and youth and is working on a commission for Quest Theatre; Janice Salkeld has been a junior high/high school teacher and a program coordinator/consultant for Early Childhood Intervention Programs; Brian Drader writes for film as well as theatre, and is presently the Director of Playwriting for the National Theatre School of Canada; Marcia Johnson is an actor and librettist, and currently playwright-in-residence for Roseneath Theatre.

Most playwrights will tell you that it takes a whole team to see the work to fruition, and that includes the audience. One of the most refreshing things about writing with young audiences of any age in mind is that they will tell you — or show you — whether your work is resonating with them, if it interests them, if they care about the characters. These plays have been road-tested and survived the exciting journey.

I asked each writer to talk about that journey — why they wanted to write for this age group, how it came about, what the development process was like, how the play was received by the first audiences, whether rewrites happened because of that experience, etc. These notes by the writers can be found at the end of each script.

I am sure that teachers of young adults will find these scripts current and refreshing examples of good writing and good scene work. The plays will provoke discussion and exciting in-class explorations. For production inquiries — should you wish to stage the full play — please note that these works are fully protected by copyright, and I encourage you to contact the publisher who will put you in touch with the writer directly. Canadian playwrights are delighted to have their work produced, and are not remotely greedy. They also need to eat.

I hope you enjoy the work.

Kit Brennan
Theatre Department, Concordia University
Montreal, Quebec

In This World

by
Hannah Moscovitch

Characters

Bijou —16, blonde
Neyssa — 16

Scene One

> *Music that is rock-concert loud.*
>
> *A fight. Two girls struggle in a high school hallway. Neyssa is pushing Bijou's face to the ground. The dialogue is all but drowned out by the music.*

BIJOU: Neyssa, get off me!
Get off me, are you crazy?
Get OFF me!

> *Neyssa pushes Bijou's head down to the floor and into the floor.*

BIJOU: *(grunting, in pain)* UH! *(strangled)* GET…OFF—

> *Bijou gets Neyssa off of her and pushes her away violently. She stands back, panting. Neyssa punches Bijou in the face. Bijou goes down. Neyssa and Bijou look at each other. Bijou puts her hand to her mouth. It's cut.*
>
> *Blackout.*

Scene Two

> *An office, confined space. The two girls sit on chairs a couple of feet apart, facing the audience. They wait, not looking at each other. Finally Neyssa glances at Bijou, then away.*

NEYSSA: I get suspended
My dad'll put me through the wall
He'll *whip* me.

> *Beat.*

I got sent home for smoking one time
The smoke set off the alarms in the bathroom at my school
My old school and he

Beat.

NEYSSA: My brother?
          He backed over our cat
          My mom's cat
          And my dad?
          He broke a bottle over his head
          We were out on the patio, we heard it, the sound of that cat
          being backed over by the car
          My dad
          Goes over
          Drags him out of the car
          My brother's seat belt was still on and Dad pulls him out of
          the seat belt and pushes his face into the cat
          The dead cat with its guts out half-under the wheel
          And then he broke the bottle over his head.

BIJOU: (*looks at her*)

NEYSSA: What?

BIJOU: Your dad *won't* whip you.

NEYSSA: Yeah, he will.

BIJOU: No, he won't.

NEYSSA: Yeah, well, your parents?
          You get suspended
          They raise your allowance
          Buy you a car, some designer shit
          "Let's throw some money at the problem 'cause that's my
          little girl
          That's my little princess little girl."

BIJOU: (*sarcastic, low*) Yeah.

NEYSSA: They gonna maybe switch you schools
          Send you to Switzerland?
          Boarding school
          Go skiing March break
          Oh, look at me, I'm Paris Hilton!
          Tits on ice.

          Beat.

NEYSSA: That cat
          It had a name kind of like yours
          Topaz
          That was the cat's name
          Cute, hunh?
          Cute name

BIJOU: (*points*)

NEYSSA: Yeah?
          What?

BIJOU: Pass me the Kleenex.

> NEYSSA *throws the box of Kleenex at* BIJOU's *head.* BIJOU *catches it and takes a Kleenex out and then puts the box on the ground. She touches her nose and face with it.*

NEYSSA: Teachers
          "I do my nine to five"
          Hiding in their offices
          OH A FIGHT OH NO SO VIOLENT
          I SAW A FIGHT THIS ONE TIME ON TV, I TURNED
          IT OFF

> Beat. BIJOU *and* NEYSSA *listen for the teachers.*

NEYSSA: MR. LEPAGE? MRS. SUNDEEN?

> Beat. Still no response.

          Well, they're not coming, so here's what they're gonna say
          to me
          Neyssa, you're suspended
          Or maybe "it's about time we get you a placement at Wal-
          Mart
          Get you out of the classroom
          All that thinking!
          You need something practical
          You can learn retail, use those excellent people skills
          Plus you'll earn a credit
          Won't that be fun?
          Hm?
          Neyssa?
          Or maybe a hairdresser's?"

BIJOU: They won't say that.
They'll tell you not to *punch* people.

> *Long Beat. BIJOU concentrates on touching her face with the Kleenex. It hurts her to do this.*

NEYSSA: (*sarcastic*) Oh, poor Bijou, your pretty face.

BIJOU: Yeah, because you *punched* / me!

NEYSSA: Yeah, sorry about that
What can I say? We bring it with us
The crime, the violence
The gun violence, don't you read the newspaper?
Don't get mixed up with us people, Bijou
And for God's sake, go to the clinic
Get yourself tested
HIV, herpes
Crabs.

> *Beat*

Gonorrhea
Gonorrhea, Bijou
STIs, Bijou, pay attention
Hey
Bijou
I'm trying to help you here.
(*claps her hands loudly*)
HEY!

BIJOU: Jesus!
What!
Why are you talking to me like you don't know me
You know / me.

NEYSSA: I'm just saying
You gotta know about protection or you'll end up full of diseases
Like that girl Siobhan
Always grabbing her crotch
Those leggings she wore too tight and I swear after Phys Ed you could smell her in the locker room long after she'd gone to class

That smell like used pads
That's what it's like, people can smell it when you pass it
out / like that—

BIJOU: I know that girl, she lived on my street
She had trouble with her parents
The divorce
She threw up
That was the smell
The stomach acid?
It wasn't an STI, it was bulimia so *shut up*, all right?
Just shut up and sit there like they told you to.

NEYSSA: You ever looked in those medical textbooks?
At the photos
The herpes?
These red blisters
Full of pus
On your mm-mm
Down there?
You seen any?
You seen some down there, Bijou?
Yes?
No?
Hey, I'm talking to you.

BIJOU: *(looks at her)*

NEYSSA: Oh, I just wish I could see the doctor's face, this little girl
walks in there
This kid

BIJOU: Okay—

NEYSSA: Walks into the clinic in sneakers and her backpack
Lunch bag
Juice box
And he's all like
So cute
Looks just like my daughter
Freckles
Blonde, nice smile
So polite, please and thank you

And then you're like
"Doctor can you please test me for herpes"

BIJOU: Okay, Neyssa—

NEYSSA: And he's like "you gotta be kidding me, this kid's out there
            screwing her face off?"

BIJOU: I'm not out there screwing my face off, I'm just screwing my
            boyfriend. Is that okay, Neyssa? Can I screw my boyfriend
            with your permission, please!

            Beat.

NEYSSA: (*incredulous*) He's your—

BIJOU: He's my boyfriend, Neyssa.
            So please
            Just *sit there*
            Can you do that?
            Can you just sit there until the teachers come?

NEYSSA: That's what he's saying to you?
            He's saying he's your boyfriend?

BIJOU: Yes.

NEYSSA: (*incredulous*) Uh, Bijou
            He's not your boyfriend.

BIJOU: Yes, he is
            How would you know?

NEYSSA: 'Cause I know him.
            He's my *cousin.*

BIJOU: Neyssa, just sit there /
            We're in detention
            Shut up

NEYSSA: No
            No
            You don't get
            Men say things, Bijou
            (*mimicking*) "I'm your boyfriend and I love you"
            Hector?
            He doesn't know what those words mean

(*mimicking*) "I'm your boyfriend"
Truth is he saw you at the party and he thought
Hey, sure I like that
He's not your…!
Trust me
He's saying those words he's saying to you to three other
girls right now
One from Villa, I bet he's always macking on some Villa[1]
girl
Next time you see him he'll act all casual, he'll have his
hands all over some other girl
And you'll just be some girl he…!
Some girl
Sorry
But
Someone had to tell you.

BIJOU:　(*hard*) They won't suspend you, Neyssa
They'll expel you
For fighting
You get expelled for that, you know that, right?

　　　Beat.

Why did you punch me?
Because of Hector?

NEYSSA:　Because.

BIJOU:　Because why?

NEYSSA:　BECAUSE!

BIJOU:　BECAUSE WHY?

NEYSSA:　BECAUSE!
I don't like that kind of
I don't like skanks
Whores
In and out of Africa
My mother taught me it's not nice.

BIJOU:　Why?

1　Please substitute in the name of whatever the "enemy" school is. The teachers at each school will know.

NEYSSA: Because
           It's disrespectful to yourself.
           It's disrespectful to yourself, it's like all you want is
           attention
           You want attention that bad, join the drama club
           Throwing yourself at him

BIJOU: Right.

NEYSSA: Oh Hector
           Oh Hector oh, have a beer, my dad doesn't drink them
           Oh you choose the music, the remote's right here
           Oh Hector, can I *jerk you off* please

BIJOU: Okay this is / crazy—

NEYSSA: My mother, if you were her daughter
           She'd send you home
           Back to Jamaica
           Learn some values
           Men don't like it, they don't look at you the same
           And I hear them
           Saying shit to each other
           "I saw that movie, it was niiice"
           "You should go see it too"
           You'll get all these guys messaging you 'cause it'll go around
           that you're this huge
           Slut—

BIJOU: Okay—

NEYSSA: And it'll get worse
           Men
           You offer them a snack and they take the whole kitchen—

BIJOU: Okay, Neyssa, this is
           I'm *not* Jamaican
           I don't want to sound racist here but *come on*
           We're in North America
           This is Canada
           I'm not locked in the basement
           I won't get stoned to death for wearing a tank top
           This isn't ZAMBIA or
           I don't know

        IRAQ
        Or JAMAICA for Christ sake
        So yeah
        I had sex with him and I don't care who knows that.

NEYSSA: You don't care?

BIJOU: Tell the whole school.

NEYSSA: Your mom?
        Your dad?

BIJOU: Come on, Neyssa
        They don't...!
        You know them, they don't care what I do—

NEYSSA: Lots of people are saying it
        Sophie
        Sara
        You should watch it the things people are saying about /
        you—

BIJOU: *You're* saying them
        You're the only one saying them

NEYSSA: The girls on the team—

BIJOU: Look, I'm not ashamed of what I did
        Most girls on our team
        Maybe they don't admit it, but most of them—

NEYSSA: No.

BIJOU: Yes!
        Yes!

NEYSSA: (*sucks her teeth*)

BIJOU: ASK THEM!

NEYSSA: You're dirty, you've got a filthy mind.

BIJOU: Neyssa, it's not
        Why?
        It's not just some way that you get STIs
        It's also this way of *being* with someone

NEYSSA: (*sucks her teeth*)

BIJOU: It is!
            This is stupid
            I'm not fighting this with you

NEYSSA: Dirty.

BIJOU: No, it's not!
            I like him
            He's my *boyfriend*
            When I'm with him it feels good
            It feels good like it feels good to
            I don't know
            Run across a field
            That's why people do it
            They don't tell you that in Jamaica I guess
            In Jamaica it's not allowed
            Jamaicans are good girls like you, isn't that right, Neyssa?
            You're all good girls who keep your minds on God
            Praying to the Virgin Mary
            On your knees three times a day
            (*mimicking*) "It's not nice to do it"
            "It's not nice, it's not nice."

NEYSSA: (*stands up*)

BIJOU: Hey, why don't you just sit down!
            Sit down, because if you hit me again—

NEYSSA: What?

BIJOU: Sit down!
            Just sit down and wait for the teachers
            Why the
            Why the
            Why have they left us here alone here together, are they
            crazy?
            WE FOUGHT, WE WERE IN A FIGHT, WE'RE GONNA
            KILL EACH OTHER IN HERE!

            *Both girls stand there for a moment and look at each
            other.*

BIJOU: Did you post that thing last night?
            On my wall?

Beat.

BIJOU: You posted that thing last night, didn't you?

NEYSSA: (*lying, provoking BIJOU*) What thing?

BIJOU: You're getting expelled
           You're gonna get expelled and sent back to Lasalle[2]
           To your ghetto

NEYSSA: I don't know what you're talking about.

BIJOU: Yes, you do.

NEYSSA: (*meaning no, but insincere*) Mm-mm.

BIJOU: Great, that's great
           This is like some news story
           Next you're what?
           Gonna go get yousself a gun
           Shoot me like Columbine?
           Last week you won't talk to me, it's like I'm not there
           You act like you HATE ME I don't know why
           It's awful. I like
           Miss you
           And now you send me threats on facebook?
           You *punch me* in the hallway?
           Why did I even
           It was like *charity*
           I invited you over to my house in September, I was like
           that poor kid they bus in from Lasalle to Westmount
           No basketball here
           It's tennis, have you seen a tennis court before?
           Your cheap clothes your cheap phone
           You talk so proud about Jamaica
           It's a shithole
           It's the Third World
           Jamaicans
           They come here, work as janitors
           And you're all proud of yourself
           "I'm Jamaican"
           "I'm a Jamaican."

2 Please substitute in the name of the 'bad' school in this district. There are two references to Lasalle on this page.

"I have values."

NEYSSA: Yeah, well, I'd rather be a Jamaican than a…!

            Beat.

BIJOU: What?

            Beat.

(*softer, longing*) Neyssa…!
I don't even know why we're fighting
I don't even know what I've done
If you didn't want me to date him you should have said that
I wouldn't have dated him
You're my
Well you were
My friend

            Beat.

I don't know why you're not happy that he and I
I wish you were happy about it, I am
I mean, you know him, he's your family, he's so…
He's just like you, he's beautiful, he's got a beautiful mind
He said this thing to me about how he likes the shape of me
It's stupid but I feel all these emotions wash over me when
I'm around him
Like, you know my house, it's this huge box with seven
bathrooms
And my mom's so busy I hang out mostly with the
housekeeper
It sounds like a joke but it's not, it's actually
My life
I'm proud of her but
Well, you see it, you're at my house, there's no one there
My dad's not much better, on business trip after business
trip
I lose track
Hong Kong, LA
He's always calling me from some airport
And I'm eating my dinner with the housekeeper and
screaming into the phone at him while he talks to me from
Korea

"Are you okay, sweetie?"
"Oh, sorry, you're breaking up"
But Hector
He calls, says can I come over?
It is not like anything else in my life, I have never had
someone who wants to just hang out with me, Neyssa
He comes over
He came over three times in the last four days and we
watched movies together, it's not like some dirty
I swear to you it's not.

NEYSSA: Yeah, well—

BIJOU: If you just saw what we're like together—

NEYSSA: *Oh,* I saw.
            At the party.

            Tense beat.

            What?
            That wasn't you?
            Showing him those photographs?

BIJOU: Fine
            Fine.

NEYSSA: You don't even *know* the guy
            We show up at your house
            And you
            Hector's my cousin, I bring him to your house
            My cousin, okay?
            I bring him, I say to him
            This is the girl, the one on my volleyball team, the one I'm
            always at her house
            She's having a party
            Come meet her
            She's this *nice girl*
            And I'm all wanting to introduce you 'cause you're my
            friend and he's my cousin
            And we show up
            And it's, oh, I happen to have shots of myself lying around
            like some porn star
            It's cheap

It's cheap behaviour
Canada Jamaica
I think that's cheap.

BIJOU: Yeah, fine
Someone took photos of me that / showed my—

NEYSSA: Those photos were / cheap, Bijou—

BIJOU: No, listen—

NEYSSA: Come on, those photos / were…!

BIJOU: Listen, I am trying to…!
It's hard enough to feel like you're not ugly and you're the
same
You are
We're both in the locker room looking at ourselves, at all
the bad parts
So I let that kid from art class take a photo of my back
I'm trying to
I don't know
Be positive about how I look—

NEYSSA: Oh, so that's why you need some porn of yourself?
To make you feel better about / your—

BIJOU: It's not porn
It's an art photo.

NEYSSA: It's a photograph of your ass hanging out the back of a
curtain which—

BIJOU: That is not / true—

NEYSSA: Which you showed to Hector the first time you met him.

BIJOU: Yeah!
Because I just got / them!

NEYSSA: I say, Bijou, this is Hector
My cousin
I grew up with him
We were kids, played together
Practically my brother
He's my one family member that I actually want you
to…!

And then you don't even remember his name
I have to tell you again in the hallway
You're like "Ooooh, right, right, Hector, I knew it began
with H"
And then next thing you're showing Hector *photos of your
ass*
You're all acting all cheap with him, *he's my cousin!*
Showing him around the house
It's just like you to
You see things, you take them
You're just like, oh that's mine and that's mine and that's
mine and that's mine

BIJOU: (*low*) Shut up.

NEYSSA: And that's mine and that's mine and that's mine and that's
mine!
You're not even noticing that I'm

    Beat.

Yeah, where did you go?

    Beat.

BIJOU: Neyssa!

NEYSSA: NOWHERE. I WAS RIGHT THERE.

BIJOU: You took off.
We tried to find you
We talked to people at the party
They were drunk. They said you left
I talked to Frank
What?
Then this week
Sending me shit on facebook
Hector keeps saying give her time to get used to it but

    Beat.

Jesus, Neyssa
My face hurts
You *punched me*
What were you thinking?

WHERE ARE THE TEACHERS?
I'm going to go and get them, I'm not sitting here anymore.

NEYSSA: (*low*) Sit down.
           Wait.

BIJOU: Why?

NEYSSA: 'Cause that's what people do, they wait for what's coming.
           Sit down!
           Wait, Bijou
           You can't get yourself out of every situation you don't like
           Just sit there and wait like a normal person.

BIJOU: Why?

NEYSSA: Things happen, Bijou, that you can't pay your way out of,
           so just sit there and wait for it.

BIJOU: My nose
           My face hurts.

NEYSSA: Yeah well, shit happens.

BIJOU: Shit happens?
           Shit happens?
           You punched me for NO REASON.

NEYSSA: I punched you because you're a slut.

                 Beat.

           Sit down.

                 Beat.

           What?
           Being hit in the face is the worst thing that's happened to
           you?
           Sit down.

BIJOU: (*sits*) Yeah, well
           From what I saw I wasn't the only one who
           At the party
           But fine.

NEYSSA: (*looks at* BIJOU)

BIJOU: Oh, what, now you're mad? Well, why don't you hit me?
Whatever
You just called me a slut
I don't call you a n(igger)…
Well, I don't.
It's the same.
So don't call me a slut.

    Beat.

What?
Why are you so angry?
What do you have to be so angry about?
No one hit *you.*
What?

    Beat.

At the party I saw you with Frank
Yeah
So I guess you think it's fine to come onto my ex
Hey whatever you can have him
Wait till you meet his parents, they live on my street
Their stupid house
Monster house
You think my house is big, just wait till you see his room
With this TV
High Def
It's like the whole wall
But hey, he's nice he's cute, I think you should go for it
I mean, you've heard all about him, I talked about him enough
He was my first real boyfriend
But hey
Go
Date my ex
I'm fine with it
And I guess you are too, I saw you with him
He's sitting all close
Had his hands on your…
Well he did.
And you weren't saying no.

Well I guess you were but there's "no" and then there's "no"
And you weren't saying "no"
You were saying "no"
(*as though flirting*) "Oh no, Frank, no
Don't do that you so bad
Oh stop, oh please"
Pretending to be all shy and not knowing what's happening
"Oh, is he hitting on me?"
"Really? I didn't notice."
Come on, you know what I'm talking about
You know he looks at you and that's fine, I guess.
That's just fine, sitting there on his lap as long as you don't actually do anything it's okay to fake it?
Sorry, I'm just trying to understand what the rules are here.

> *Beat.*

What?

NEYSSA: Nothing.

BIJOU: What!
Why are you looking at me like…?

NEYSSA: I'm not looking at you.

BIJOU: What
Did he
What happened?
I saw you guys, you were sitting on the couch together when we went upstairs
What?

NEYSSA: Nothing!

BIJOU: Well, something happened because you're
Where did you go?
You were in the house?
I looked for you—

NEYSSA: Yeah?

BIJOU: Yeah!
I looked for you!

NEYSSA: You check the basement?

BIJOU: That's where you were?
            Down in the basement?

NEYSSA: I got the grand tour.

BIJOU: (*low*) Did you
            Did you
            With Frank?!
            In my basement?

NEYSSA: Yeah, not quite
            But thanks
            Thanks for leaving me alone with your ex
            Thanks for going off with my cousin and leaving me alone
            with Frank so he could lock me in your basement.

BIJOU: What!
            He
            What!
            What happened?

NEYSSA: Nothing.

BIJOU: No, what do you mean he locked you?

NEYSSA: I mean he locked me in your basement!

BIJOU: Why?

NEYSSA: (*shrugs*) I don't know!

BIJOU: You don't know why?

NEYSSA: No!

            Beat.

            He goes down there
            Calls me
            Saying
            Come down here
            So…!
            I walk down
            He locks the door takes the key
            And he's all joking

"Come here, come here, I have the key"
"Come get the key"
And I'm like "okay, I'll let him kiss me
I'll just let him, it's fine, he's nice"
I'm not wanting to be
Rude
And I like him enough and the party up there is filled with people I don't know getting wasted
So I'm with him down there trying to, I don't know
Relax
But it turned into this
Fight
This
It turned
He was drunk and he kept saying "come here, oh, I'm stronger than you"
And it's just, it turns, it's almost like he's still joking but I'm
Trying to
I go to the door and I pound on it
Some people from the party come down, they hear me pounding
Not *you*, though
Not you or Hector

BIJOU: What.

NEYSSA: I lived in
It's crazy
Lots of places that
Shitty back rooms behind stores
Motels
Those places when we first moved here
And I walk home by myself at night and nothing's ever gone wrong
Then I come to your house
Your party
Hector and you just upstairs just ten feet from me in the basement

BIJOU: Wait—

NEYSSA:	Just through the ceiling On the other side of the / wall—
BIJOU:	Wait What happened?
NEYSSA:	Nothing. All right? Nothing Nothing would have happened if you hadn't gone off with Hector.
BIJOU:	Wait a second You were in the basement and…? Neyssa, you have to tell me what happened.
NEYSSA:	I JUST DID.

Beat.

BIJOU:	Are you saying Are you saying he—
NEYSSA:	No.
BIJOU:	Are you saying Frank *raped* you?
NEYSSA:	No, I am not saying that Are you listening? Listen to me, I'm saying where were you? *Where were you?* Okay? When I was in the basement? Oh wait. Upstairs. Screwing my cousin. Yeah. That's what I'm saying.
BIJOU:	Okay okay wait a sec You're saying *something* happened down there And you went along with it? But you're not saying…?
NEYSSA:	(*looks at her*)

BIJOU: Oh my God.
Oh my God
I mean
I know Frank, I dated him for a whole year
I've known him my whole life
We
He
He's Frank!
I mean, he likes to get his own way but he was never even
a little crossing the line with me—

NEYSSA: Forget it.

BIJOU: Maybe he didn't realize that you...?

NEYSSA: FORGET IT
LIKE I SAID.

BIJOU: I mean, are you saying he didn't listen to you or he wanted
you to when you didn't want / it—

NEYSSA: I'M SAYING FORGET IT, OKAY?
FORGET IT
YOU JUST GO ON SCREWING MY COUSIN
You WHORE.
You slut. *(covers her eyes, tries not to cry)*

BIJOU: Neyssa.

> *Beat.* NEYSSA'*s head is down.* BIJOU *touches her to comfort her.*

(*softly*) Neyssa.
Don't
Don't cry
Don't—

NEYSSA: I'm not!

BIJOU: Neyssa.

NEYSSA: It's fine!
Like I said, it's fine
I just don't want to talk about it.

BIJOU: You
It's not fine

NEYSSA: It is fine!
            It's fine
            I just wanted Hector to
            Punch that guy
            But where is he, he's with you somewhere up in your *stupid
            house—*

BIJOU: Neyssa.

NEYSSA: Your *stupid...*!
            You *left* me.
            You know I don't know those people
            You're my one friend at this
            Stupid school
            You get me drunk and then you leave me there, you could
            see Frank was hitting on me and I'm saying no to him and
            you just
            Left me.

                    Beat.

BIJOU: (*low*) Oh my God I'm sorry.

NEYSSA: And then I get out of there
            And you and Hector are *nowhere*
            And Frank is still at the party, he's in the kitchen
            So I go home
            I walked home alone in the streets, it was nice
            I thought
            What
            After all
            Can happen to me now?

BIJOU: Shit, Neyssa
            Shit, I'm sorry I'm
            Sorry
            Are you okay?
            Like physically are you...?
            Neyssa?

NEYSSA: It was like a week-and-a half ago now.
            There's nothing
            I
            Went and got a Plan B from this walk-in clinic

So
Nothing
Just
Nothing
Bruises.

BIJOU: This is so crazy
Like he actually
Why would he do that?
It's so *stupid*
That's his whole life he / just—

NEYSSA: His whole life?
No.
Why?

BIJOU: Because he…!

NEYSSA: No one will know.

BIJOU: Yes, they will.

NEYSSA: No.
How?

BIJOU: When the teachers come you have to tell / them—

NEYSSA: The teachers?
No

BIJOU: Neyssa
You have to say something
You have to—

NEYSSA: No.

BIJOU: Neyssa—

NEYSSA: No!

The girls look at each other.

NEYSSA: Oh, what? Now you want to tell on him?
Your first boyfriend?
"I've known him my whole life?"

BIJOU: I'm sorry— I
He's my ex, I still

It's just hard to see him as a
Rapist
But if he hurt you—

NEYSSA: He didn't.

BIJOU: Yes he did.

            Beat.

            Yes he did.

NEYSSA: And what?
            It happened.

BIJOU: So you have to tell someone.

NEYSSA: No I don't.

BIJOU: Yes you do.

NEYSSA: No I don't.
            Why?

BIJOU: Because of what he did!

NEYSSA: Nothing happened.
            I keep saying nothing happened, forget it.

BIJOU: I'll tell them.

NEYSSA: No!
            You won't.

BIJOU: Yes I will.

NEYSSA: No you won't.

BIJOU: Neyssa!

NEYSSA: No!
            My life is
            Already it's
            Just to try and *be* in this world is
            My mother is not a lawyer, Bijou, she's at Pharmaprix

BIJOU: Neyssa—

NEYSSA: NO
            WHAT?

YOU DON'T KNOW
I am the light of my mother's life
I am the light
I go to this school
I go here, I got grades high enough to get me here
My mother
She has enough things that are wrong
I can't tell her "oh you fought so hard, you brought me here to give me things, but I'm sorry it didn't work because look what's happened to me"
My brother is the disappointment of her life, okay?
But me, I'm like this *beacon*
She thinks I'm going to be a doctor and *save the Jamaican people* or something, okay?
I can't tell her
And that's fine, I don't want to tell her, I don't want to tell anyone
I just don't want to stay at this school
I hate this school
I just want to go back to my old school—

BIJOU: Neyssa, you have to tell Mrs. Sundeen—

NEYSSA: Why?
           You think I should tell the teachers
           Why?

BIJOU: Because they'll help, they'll know what to do—

NEYSSA: Because that's what we're supposed to do?
           That's what they taught you?

BIJOU: Yeah, because—

NEYSSA: You do everything the teachers tell you to!

BIJOU: No, but you / were raped!

NEYSSA: What do you think they're gonna do?
           They're adults, they're not Superman.
           They can't fix it
           They can't undo it
           It's too late for parents and teachers now, this is the real
           Shit happens, Bijou.

BIJOU: Neyssa, I am telling the teachers—

NEYSSA: No you are not.

BIJOU: Neyssa—

NEYSSA: No
I do not want this to be
My life

BIJOU: Neyssa

NEYSSA: I want to just forget it

BIJOU: Neyssa

NEYSSA: What!
IF YOU HAD TURNED DOWN YOUR STUPID
SPEAKERS YOU WOULD HAVE HEARD ME, I WAS

           Beat.

           (*lowered voice*) Yelling down there.

           Beat.

           I walked to school this morning
           The river was frozen and I had this thought, it kept
           I wanted to go out on the ice
           In the middle where it's thin it's all black
           I had a cigarette there by the bridge
           Thinking
           I could just smoke this cigarette and then walk out there
           onto the ice…

BIJOU: Neyssa—

NEYSSA: No
What?
It's fine, I'm fine, I just have to get out of this school.

           Beat.

           It's funny, you know what's funny
           I kind of liked him
           The way he looked at me today
           He looks like he's not sure what happened
           And I'm not either 'cause what did I say?

I know I didn't say nothing but I don't know if I said the
right things

BIJOU: You did.

NEYSSA: No because at first I thought it was this
Joke
I don't know if I said soon enough
What if I didn't?
At first, upstairs at the party, I was saying no and it didn't
mean no, it meant maybe
Could he even tell the difference between when I meant it
and when I didn't?

BIJOU: Yeah he could
Neyssa, we have got to tell someone.
We are telling someone who will tell you it's not your
fault
A teacher, or I'll go to emergency with you, talk to
someone—

NEYSSA: Jesus. I said no.

BIJOU: Oh my God
Neyssa, please don't be crazy
We are telling a doctor at least—

NEYSSA: And where were you?
Hunh?
With your "tell a doctor"
I go home, you don't even call me—

BIJOU: (low) I'm sorry
I'm sorry—

NEYSSA: Yeah
That's what's going to happen, everyone is going to be
sorry
"I'm so sorry, Neyssa"
"I'm so sorry about that, I'm sorry this happened, we're so
sorry"
I don't want to be that girl who / got—

BIJOU: Okay, fine, but Neyssa, it won't be like that for / you—

NEYSSA: Oh yes it will, I know a girl
            I heard about her my whole life, she lives in my
            neighborhood
            She never got over it and we all know her as that girl who
            Oh, that's the girl
            A bunch of guys, they dragged her into a park and she
            never got over it.

BIJOU: Neyssa—

NEYSSA: Men don't like it
            They don't look at you the same.

BIJOU: It won't be like that
            Everyone, they'll all take your side
            But we have to—

NEYSSA: What?

BIJOU: Tell someone!

NEYSSA: NO!

BIJOU: It's okay.
            We won't tell the teachers
            Just my mom, she knows lawyers who deal with these sort
            of—

NEYSSA: No

BIJOU: No, listen—

NEYSSA: No
            I don't want you to.
            That is my choice
            That is my choice, Bijou
            Okay?
            That's what I want, I want it to *be over*—

BIJOU: Neyssa—

NEYSSA: Listen to what I'm saying—

BIJOU: At least let me tell my mom—

NEYSSA: No.

BIJOU: You have to—

NEYSSA: No I don't.

BIJOU: At least tell *Hector*—

NEYSSA: Come on, Bijou, don't be stupid, he'll tell *my mom.*

BIJOU: Neyssa, please, for God's sake
            You're going to need it
            It will
            You can't get away from something like this, it's too big—

NEYSSA: Sure I can.

BIJOU: You can't just handle this yourself, Neyssa
            You need someone to help you, this is crazy
            I'm not fighting this with you
            If you got shot, if someone shot you in the stomach and
            you wanted to operate on it yourself, I would say no
            Come on!
            It's a serious medical
            You cannot pretend that it isn't

NEYSSA: It isn't, I'm fine
            Look at me
            There's nothing wrong with me.

BIJOU: What are you talking about?
            You're acting crazy
            You punched me
            That's you being fine?

NEYSSA: No—

BIJOU: You're not fine.
            We are getting someone right now and telling / them—

NEYSSA: No, I punched you because
            I have to get out of this school
            I have to
            I keep seeing him in the *hallway*
            I can't stay here
            They have to expel me
            All you have to do is tell them I punched you and I'll get
            expelled

And that's the truth
That's what happened
I punched you
So just tell the truth, that's what I want

BIJOU: You want to get expelled?

NEYSSA: Yeah.

BIJOU: But, Neyssa, that's stupid
He'll get expelled.

NEYSSA: No he won't

BIJOU: Yes he will
He will get expelled for that.

NEYSSA: NO ONE SAW IT
YOU DIDN'T SEE IT
THERE IS NOTHING.

      Beat.

Look, just pretend I didn't tell you.

      BIJOU stands and walks towards the door.

BIJOU: No, this is crazy
He raped you.

NEYSSA: No, he didn't
Like I said, it wasn't like that.

BIJOU: Yes, he did!

NEYSSA: Sit down.
Sit down!

BIJOU: I am
Telling
Someone.
Neyssa

NEYSSA: *(advancing towards BIJOU)* No
You
No

      NEYSSA gets hold of her.

BIJOU: NEYSSA!

NEYSSA: SIT DOWN.

BIJOU: I am telling someone!

NEYSSA: No
            I'll
            I'll kill you.
            I'll

BIJOU: Neyssa

NEYSSA: I'll

BIJOU: Please.

NEYSSA: I'll *kill you.*

BIJOU: Please, I
            Come on, I will feel so bad
            My ex
            In my basement
            And I'm upstairs with your
            Neyssa
            Please, I will have to live with that

NEYSSA: So?
            I have to live with it.

> NEYSSA takes BIJOU's hands. They stand together, quite still.

NEYSSA: Please just for *one second* stop thinking about what you're
            supposed to do in this
            Situation
            And think about my life
            About what I want
            Listen to me, I'm right here
            I am saying I don't want to tell anyone
            I want it to just
            Be over
            Come on, I'm just asking you this one thing.

> Beat.

NEYSSA: Just
             Please
             Be my friend
             Okay?

             Beat.

NEYSSA: Okay?

BIJOU: (*soft*) Okay.
             Okay.
             I won't tell.

             Beat.

             I won't tell.

NEYSSA: Just tell them that I hit you, okay?

BIJOU: Yeah
             Okay
             I'll do what you want
             I won't tell.
             I'll just let you—

NEYSSA: That's what I want.

BIJOU: Okay well then that's what I'll do.
             It's okay.
             Don't worry.
             Don't worry, it's fine, it's going to be fine.
             I'm sorry.
             It's fine.
             It's okay.
             Shh.

             *BIJOU puts her arms around NEYSSA and holds her,
             rocks her.*

             The End

Production Credits

In This World opened at Théâtre Calixa-Lavallée on the 16th of March, 2009 with the following cast and crew:

Produced by	Youtheatre
Director	Michel Lefebvre
Set and Costumes	Véronique Bertrand
Lighting	Renaud Pettigrew
Music	Martin Messier
Bijou	Hannah Cheesman
Neyssa	Sharon James
Study Guide	Janna Smith

Research and development work in participation with Lasalle Community Comprehensive and École secondaire Jean XXIII

Acknowledgements

I am deeply indebted to Michel Lefebvre, who acted as dramaturge as well as director on the project. I'd like to thank the two actors who workshopped the script, Hannah Cheesman and Adrienne Irving, and the two actors who premiered the play, Hannah Cheesman and Sharon James. My thanks are also due to the students at Lasalle Community Comprehensive and École secondaire Jean XXIII who agreed to let me interview them while I was researching the project. The writing of *In This World* was made possible through a playwright-in-residence grant from The Canada Council for the Arts.

About the Playwright

Hannah Moscovitch is an emerging artist who has been dubbed "an indie sensation" by *Toronto Life* magazine, "the wunderkind of Canadian theatre" by CBC Radio, and "irritatingly talented" by *Eye Weekly*. Hannah's past writing for the stage includes her short works *Essay*, *The Russian Play*, *USSR*, and *Mexico City*, and her Dora nominated full-length play, *East of Berlin*. Hannah's plays have been produced across the country, including at the Tarragon Theatre in Toronto where she is currently playwright-in-residence, the Factory Theatre, Alberta Theatre Projects and the Magnetic North Theatre Festival. Hannah is a graduate of The National Theatre School of Canada's acting program and she attended the University of Toronto.

Interview

My impulse to write *In This World* came from the desire to speak about authentic teenage experience. When I was a teenager I saw plays about how suicide is wrong or racism is bad. These plays were instructive but they weren't compelling. They told what I already knew — adults think suicide is wrong — but they didn't speak about why teenagers might legitimately want to kill themselves. I couldn't connect those plays to my friend lying on the floor outside the bathroom at a party, puking vodka coolers into a frying pan we'd found in the kitchen, telling me that she wished she was dead because her mom was dying of cancer and her father cried every night all through dinner. When I was in high school, I was in the first throes of learning that the world is complex and that ethical terra firma is elusive, and so simple dictums like "suicide is bad" already seemed empty to me. I wrote *In This World* because I wanted to create a play for the teenager I was.

There is no difference that I can discern between my writing for teenagers and my work for a general audience. It occurs to me to say that *In This World* features teenage characters but then so do many of my plays for adults. Michel Lefebvre, the executive director of Youtheatre, encouraged me to write in my own voice and so I didn't try to write a play for young audiences.

What drew me to this material in particular was Michel Lefebvre's offer; he suggested I write him a play about female teenage sexuality. I felt like I had something to say about the topic. In the Sex Ed discourse of the 90s, when I was growing up, I was told loudly and clearly that I had the right to say no to sex. I was never told I had the right to say yes. The possibility that a girl might want to say yes to sex was strangely absent from the dialogue. Female desire was never talked about, and girls my age didn't admit to feeling any. I heard girls justify their sex lives by claiming to be drunk, "I was so loaded I didn't know what I was doing," or in love, "I let him because I love him." I never heard girls say, "I wanted to do it." This was at a time when the women's movement was taking back the night and condoms were being dispensed in high school bathrooms. What initially drew me to writing *In This World* was the disconnection between the atmosphere of sexual liberation and the female teen denial of sexuality.

Michel and I developed the play through a series of interviews with teenage girls. I had a general sense of what I wanted to write about but I needed something more specific and more current. Michel drove me to two schools in the Montreal area, and I interviewed a group of girls at each of them. The first interview group was dominated by three Jamaican girls who told me that, "men like what's fresh, they like raw meat" and they won't look at you twice if you're not a virgin, that blow jobs are "dirty" and that sex is something you don't just give away. They revealed over the course of the interview that they were saving themselves, if not for marriage, then for some distant later date, and that they had once beat up a girl for "slutting." They were wholly untouched by the feminism of the 70s that had so completely dominated my upbringing. The second group was the reverse. They were mostly Quebecois kids from "the dirts" as they called it. The most outspoken girl of the group said right off the bat, "yeah, I've had sex with two guys and I don't care who knows it." In this group it was the virgins who had to justify themselves and it was the more sexually active girls who were the pretty, popular, powerful ones. I became interested in the possibility of putting the alpha girl from each of the two schools onstage together, and just letting them have it out. From that impulse came the play.

The title *In This World* is a line taken from the script. I wanted the title to encapsulate the reason why Neyssa makes the choice she does at the end of the play.

Offensive Fouls

by
Jason Long

Characters

CHRISTINE — 17, Chinese
JOEY — 17, Caucasian

Time

Spring

Place

A somewhat run-down, infrequently used suburban park. Asphalt basketball court/hoop indicated off. Metal garbage can. Park bench.

Playwright's Notes

Joey's opening monologue references actual NBA basketball players. Knowing that this is the age of free agency and team rosters are constantly in flux, please feel free to change/update the names in keeping with the current rosters at the time of production. (In this final version, I'm using Boston Celtic players. Joey digs the Celtic — Irish! — so keeping the Celtics as his team would be optimal but not required.)

Due to a casting issue, a prior production of this play changed Christine from Chinese heritage to Indian (South Asian). If producers run across this issue in the future, I would be more than happy—in conjunction with the theatre company—to make alterations to the script in order to satisfy these potential dilemmas.

Suburban park, late afternoon, spring. SOUND of basketball bouncing in blackout.

Lights up. CHRISTINE, *17, sits on the park bench, arms folded, staring straight ahead. Bouncing gets louder as* JOEY, *17, enters, bouncing the ball, pretending to be guarded by a defender.*

JOEY: …See at this point he knows. He KNOWS, ya know? Paul Pierce, The Truth, he knows all. Dribbling in the paint, defence scurries, seconds goin' tick-tick-tick… Other team thinks he's hesitatin', unsure, back to the bucket. The guy defendin' him—can't remember his name, some mook, some hack—tries a few pansy slaps at the ball but he can't get to Pierce. I mean, the guy's an oak tree on wheels, right? So… He looks to K.G., looks to the hoop, takes a step. Looks to K.G., to Allen, to the hoop, another step. Shifts the ball to his left hand. K.G., Allen, hoop, the clock… Pivots left, stops, cuts back right, bam! *(makes swinging motion with right elbow)* Chump defender goes down, Pauly fades a beauty ten-footer, and that's game over! *(imitates the shot, makes buzzer sound, ball falls and rolls)* Paul Pierce, he is SO the man. Playoff b-ball, I love this game.

JOEY looks to CHRISTINE, *who remains, arms folded, staring off. Beat.*

JOEY: Good game an' all, but I can't stand watchin' sports with my brother and dad. Both a' them got on me—again—'bout goin' to University in the fall, gettin' into Phys Ed, thinkin' I'm a lock to make the basketball team. I mean, I know I'm a good player an' all. Certain aspects of my game are solid, anyway. Outside shot, good vision—meaning I see the court well. *(beat)* Good *game* vision, not like my eyesight's better than anyone else's. I mean my eyesight's good, twenty-twenty last check-up… Anyway. Dad n' Doyle have been pushin' hard, but I keep tellin' them no way. I'm takin' the year off, me an' Christine got our trip to Europe in the fall so school's out of the question. But they don't get it. I mean, yeah, I could prob'ly make the team eventually, but come on, like bein' on some joe Canadian university b-ball team's gonna vault me to the pro's. That's what they think! Can you believe that?

JOEY looks to CHRISTINE again. She's still staring off.
Beat.

JOEY: I don't think the old man's ever pulled in his life, you
        know? Just push push push! I remember when I was a
        kid, three-four years old, the guy wouldn't even go into
        a public washroom with me. Open the door, push me in,
        "Be quick, Joe!" I didn't know what a urinal was until I
        was ten years old! Doyle was the one who set me straight,
        like I've ever heard the end a' that story, no way. Older
        brothers, man. They always remember. Every stupid little
        thing you did as a kid, every time you fell on your face or
        picked up dog crap and asked, "Hey, what kinda rock is
        this?" Every little…

        JOEY looks to CHRISTINE again. She's still staring off.
        Beat. He cautiously sits down next to her.

JOEY: So how was your day?… Couldn't find you. Not at your
        locker, in the caf, library… Were you hidin' from me or
        somethin'?

        JOEY makes a nervous, forced laugh. No response from
        CHRISTINE. He clears his throat, continues.

JOEY: You look tired. Get much sleep last night?… You coulda
        called me. I was up late. Tossin' and turnin'. The moon
        musta been, you know, whatever. Somethin'… *(pause,*
        chuckles) Had the *weirdest* dream last night. With you
        in it, of course. We went to the travel agent to book our
        plane tickets, right, except the agency was in some tuxedo
        rental shop in the gym at school. Before I could even talk
        to the person at the counter—who was one a' them freaky
        mimes—you know me n' mimes, eh?—you flipped out at
        me for no reason because I wasn't in "formal attire." *(over-*
        the-top laugh) Isn't that insane? You getting pissy at me
        was funny enough, you know…'cuz you never do…but
        because I wasn't dressed up enough for the travel agent?
        How whack is that, eh?… Eh?…

        Nothing. JOEY clears his throat again, getting sweaty.

JOEY: I like that shirt… New?… Great colours. Bold… *(pause)*
        Oh. You were right, by the way. That fancy pencil you lent

me works way better than regular ones. I keep snapping the lead thingys though, but hey, it beats having to sharpen every five minutes, right?... Right?... So thanks... For the...pencil... Thank you...

> *CHRISTINE doesn't stir. Beat. JOEY stands up, starts to dribble the ball again.*

JOEY: In the first quarter, Pierce drew two fouls back-to-back 'cause the defenders were—

> *CHRISTINE jumps to her feet, grabs the ball away from him.*

JOEY: What?

> *CHRISTINE bounces the ball off JOEY's forehead, catches it.*

JOEY: Why'd you—?

> *She does it again.*

JOEY: Hey, stop—

> *Again.*

JOEY: All right, what—?

> *She does it again, but JOEY blocks the ball, drops it back into her hands.*

JOEY: Aha!

> *CHRISTINE shoves the ball in JOEY's stomach. He lets out a huge groan, gasps for air.*

JOEY: Nice pass. On the money.

CHRISTINE: *(calm, controlling her anger)* You are a sad, stupid, unfunny, uninteresting little boy with a weird, misshaped head and a nose that whistles when you walk upwind.

JOEY: I—

CHRISTINE: Shut up. The only thing worse than watching some pointless basketball game on TV is listening to you re-create it the next day.

JOEY: I didn't mean to—

CHRISTINE: Shut up. I heard you the first time, when you told me your dad and brother were pushing you to go to university. I heard you the first time—four months ago! I do not need to hear it repeated by you with your nasal, preschool girl voice every day.

JOEY: Preschool girl?

CHRISTINE: Shut up.

JOEY: Last week you said my voice sounded like that "hot" beer commercial guy. With the beard.

CHRISTINE: I lied, idiot.

JOEY: Why would you lie about that?

CHRISTINE: You paid for the movie, figured I'd be nice.

JOEY: Why—?

> *CHRISTINE clamps JOEY's mouth shut with her hand, holds it.*

CHRISTINE: No more squeaking, little girl. Number one on the list of things I NEVER need to hear from you again is that it wasn't until you were ten years old that you figured out what a urinal was! You are whiney, you are boring, you've worn that T-shirt three times this week, and put your stupid hat on your pointy head properly!

> *CHRISTINE takes her hand away, sits on the bench. JOEY puts his hat on straight—backwards. Confused. Beat.*

JOEY: So where were you all day?

CHRISTINE: Why don't I ask you a question?

JOEY: Okay.

CHRISTINE: Would you mind?

JOEY: No.

CHRISTINE: You sure?

JOEY: That'd be great.

CHRISTINE: Have you noticed I'm a little…oh…not quite myself today?

JOEY: Yeah.

CHRISTINE: You've noticed?

JOEY: Yeah. You seem kinda…I dunno…cross.

CHRISTINE: Cross?

JOEY: Yeah, cross. Like, not happy.

CHRISTINE: So you've noticed my crossness?

JOEY: Kinda hard not to.

CHRISTINE: Were you ever going to inquire about my crossness at
           some point?

JOEY: I dunno. I've never really—

CHRISTINE: What?

JOEY: I never seen you this cross before so I was sorta…scared to
           bring it up.

CHRISTINE: Scared why?

JOEY: 'Cause I figgered I did somethin' to make you…cross.

CHRISTINE: Why would you think that?

JOEY: Well, your repeated bouncin' the ball off my head got me
           thinkin'.

CHRISTINE: Did it hurt?

JOEY: Little surprised but not—

CHRISTINE: Not the bouncing, Joey, the "thinkin." Was that very
           painful for you? To think?

JOEY: *(pause)* See, that right there makes me think you might be
           mad at me.

CHRISTINE: What did you do yesterday?

JOEY: I told you, I watched the game with—

CHRISTINE: The whole day, run down the whole day.

JOEY: I got up, I had breakfast, went to school—

CHRISTINE: Skip ahead.

JOEY: —Hung out with you, had dinner, watched the ball game, did a little homework, phoned you, went to bed.

CHRISTINE: That's it?

JOEY: Okay I didn't really "do" homework but—

CHRISTINE: Did you have any snacks while you watched the game?

JOEY: Snacks? Yeah, I guess. Chips an' stuff.

CHRISTINE: Did you run out at some point? Needed more, so you went out and…bought more snacks?

JOEY: Uh…don't think so.

CHRISTINE: You did or you didn't, which is it?

JOEY: Didn't, then.

CHRISTINE: Your brother? Did he go out for snacks?

JOEY: *(touches his stomach)* Is this your way of sayin' I should cut back on eating between meals or somethin'?

CHRISTINE: Did you, your brother, father, mother, cousins, anyone at anytime leave your house last night?

JOEY: Maybe. I can't account for my whole family, y'know. Why are you hasslin' me about snacks?

CHRISTINE: I was given some rather interesting information this morning.

JOEY: About snacks?

CHRISTINE: Are you sure you weren't out of your house last night?

JOEY: Yeah, I'm sure, I mean, maybe, I dunno, I might have…

CHRISTINE: What?

JOEY: Hang on, I'm thinkin'.

CHRISTINE: So this could take awhile.

JOEY: Geez, Chris! What the…? Could you please stop insultin' me and tell me what's goin' on?

CHRISTINE: I need to know, tell me… Tell me the truth.

JOEY: Have I ever lied to you before?

CHRISTINE: No.

JOEY: So why would I start now?

CHRISTINE: Did you go to Chan's Snack Shop at any time last night?

JOEY: Chan's?

CHRISTINE: Did you?

JOEY: No.

CHRISTINE: You're sure?

JOEY: No. I mean, yes, I'm sure that no I wasn't at Chan's yesterday.

CHRISTINE: Really?

JOEY: Yes really!

CHRISTINE hugs JOEY, holds him. Beat.

CHRISTINE: I'm sorry.

JOEY: Okay.

CHRISTINE: I didn't mean to... I should've... I'm sorry.

JOEY: It's okay, Chris.

They kiss.

JOEY: Boy. That's better.

CHRISTINE: Yeah.

They sit, arms around each other, smiling.

JOEY: Hey, you have that bio quiz today? More proof Mister Taylor's the biggest douche on the planet. Guy actually docked me half a mark 'cause I put the wrong date at the top of my paper. The frickin' date, I mean... The guy's got it in for me.

CHRISTINE: Last night some guys were in Mister Chan's store, they got into a big argument with him.

JOEY: Oh yeah?

CHRISTINE: Got pretty bad. They knocked over merchandise, and said some...some pretty awful things to him.

JOEY: Uh, huh.

CHRISTINE: And someone told me they saw…your brother there.

JOEY: Doyle? Who told you that?

CHRISTINE: Well, they didn't exactly see him, they—

JOEY: What?

CHRISTINE: Someone heard him.

JOEY: Heard?

CHRISTINE: Heard him fighting with Mister Chan.

JOEY: Wait a minute. "Heard"? What is that?

CHRISTINE: This person wouldn't lie.

JOEY: This person is wrong. Doyle wouldn't do stuff like that, he's not…no way.

CHRISTINE: You sure?

JOEY: You don't know my brother like I do.

CHRISTINE: I know his type.

JOEY: His type? What's that mean?

CHRISTINE: Forget it. I didn't mean—

JOEY: Look, there's no frickin' way Doyle was even near Chan's last night.

CHRISTINE: How do you know?

JOEY: Because after the game on TV we went and shot hoops with… *(stops)*

CHRISTINE: Go on.

JOEY: With his buddy Shane.

CHRISTINE: So you did go out last night.

JOEY: Well, sort of. Not really "out" but—

CHRISTINE: That's one.

JOEY: What?

CHRISTINE: You told me you never left the house last night.

JOEY: I said I couldn't remember. What's the big—? I mean, walkin' down the street an' shootin' hoops at the park ain't exactly "goin' out."

CHRISTINE: So why did this slip your mind earlier?

JOEY: It didn't, I just—Geez, Chris, you were so mad at me an' I was tryin' to figure out why, I couldn't conc—So excuse me, okay? I'm sorry. Yeah, I left my house last night to play ball with my brother and his friend. Didn't realize that was a crime.

CHRISTINE walks right, looks off.

CHRISTINE: Three of you, huh?

JOEY: Yeah.

CHRISTINE: You shot hoops here?

JOEY: Yeah, so what?

CHRISTINE: Chan's is only a couple blocks away.

JOEY: Oh. So now 'cause someone apparently "heard" Doyle at Chan's last night you automatically assume I was—?

CHRISTINE: What time did you leave the house?

JOEY: *(grabs his basketball)* Screw this! *(starts off)* Some frickin' anniversary.

JOEY exits.

CHRISTINE: It's not our anniversary.

JOEY: *(off)* What?

CHRISTINE: You said anniversary, but it's not.

JOEY: *(off)* Yes it is. Six months today.

CHRISTINE: Six months today what?

JOEY: *(off)* Six months today we started goin' out. I'm sorry you don't remember. It's a pretty important day in my life.

CHRISTINE: It'll be six months next Friday.

JOEY: *(off)* You're mist… *(walks back on)* You're mistaken. Six months ago today, at Andy's party, we—

CHRISTINE: —Had an awkward, out-of-the-blue make-out session in his basement and fell asleep watching *Scooby Doo*.

JOEY: Yeah. We started goin' out then.

CHRISTINE: No because you avoided me for the next week at school, then the next Friday at Amy's I finally cornered you. You apologized, another slightly-less-awkward make-out session—this time that food dehydrator infomercial was on—and I said to you "Are we going out or what?" You paused, scratched that pointy head of yours and said "Uh… Hmm… I, uh… Sure." Six months next week, not today.

> *Pause.*

JOEY: So what's your point?

CHRISTINE: That sometimes you have moments of…forgetfulness. Mixed up our anniversary day, so isn't it possible you may have forgotten your whereabouts last night?

JOEY: I can read between the lines, your honour.

CHRISTINE: Don't get—

JOEY: No no. "Forgotten my whereabouts." I get what that is. That is fancy talk for "Joey's a liar."

CHRISTINE: You're getting—

JOEY: I'm getting tired of the third degree, that's what I'm getting, Chris! So here it is: Watched ball on TV. Shot hoops—for a *bit*—with Doyle and Shane. Went home. In my room. Rest of the night. Whatever Doyle n' Shane did after that I have no clue, but trust me. Your little informant is way off. It didn't happen.

> *JOEY shoots the ball in anger, using the garbage can as a hoop. Dribbles away from her. Slowly, CHRISTINE moves to him. Takes the ball away. Pause.*

CHRISTINE: I trust you.

JOEY: Beg your pardon?

CHRISTINE: You heard me.

JOEY: One more time, please. For the record.

CHRISTINE: I trust you. And I'm sorry. I said some things, mean things…and I shouldn't have doubted you.

JOEY: *(beat)* 'Kay.

> CHRISTINE *sidles up to him, playfully bumps his hip. Beat.*

JOEY: All that tension… Kinda put a damper on my big news.

CHRISTINE: What big news?

JOEY: Forget it. Not import—

CHRISTINE: Of course it is, tell me.

JOEY: Well…I sorta made these plans… 'Cause I thought tonight was our anniv…I was gonna take you to…

CHRISTINE: Where? Where?

JOEY: *(pause)* The King of the Dancing River Folks.

CHRISTINE: What?

JOEY: *(pulls out tickets)* The King of the Dancing River Folks. It's this big touring Irish dance show and I was gonna… Got my dad's car for the night, had my confirmation suit let out and… No biggie. If you'd rather not—

> CHRISTINE *takes the tickets. Looks at them.*

CHRISTINE: Come here.

JOEY: No.

CHRISTINE: Come here.

JOEY: I don't wanna.

> CHRISTINE *moves to* JOEY, *lifts his head, kisses him, puts her arms around him.*

CHRISTINE: Thank you.

JOEY: You're welcome… Happy not-really-our-anniversary.

CHRISTINE: We can have two anniversaries. I'll take you out next week.

JOEY: Two anniversaries. Wicked!

CHRISTINE: *(looks at tickets)* These are really expensive.

JOEY: Yeah, well... I couldn't get better than first balcony, but...
             Still think it'll be cool.

CHRISTINE: It'll be great.

             They kiss. CHRISTINE looks at the tickets.

CHRISTINE: So who are these King of the Dancing River Folks
             anyway?

JOEY: You never heard a' them? *(she shakes her head)* Aw, they're
             amazing. Huge in the States and Europe. And Spain. They
             used to be just The Dancing River Folks but the lead guy
             got in a scrap with the producers so he broke away to do
             his own thing.

CHRISTINE: So what is the show?

JOEY: Uh...dancin'. Irish dancing. For like five hours.

CHRISTINE: What is Irish dancing exactly?

JOEY: Oh, it's unlike any kinda dancin' you've ever seen! It's like
             all really slick an' choreographed, cool Celtic music playin'
             in the background. It's almost like tap dancing but...but
             Irish. Like this.

             *JOEY attempts, poorly, to demonstrate Irish dancing.
             Legs kicking up, arms rigid at his side. CHRISTINE tries
             to suppress her laughter.*

CHRISTINE: Why aren't your arms moving?

JOEY: That's what makes it Irish!

             *JOEY pushes to a fever pace, stops, wincing, grabbing his
             leg.*

             So...it's like that. But good.

CHRISTINE: And, what? Irish people dance like this all the time?

JOEY: Aw, man, in Ireland, they walk down the street like that.
             (demonstrates again, Irish accent) "La la la, hello Seamus,
             just goin' ta pick up some bread. Lovely day." They are
             a very happy, light-footed people... *(stops)* Ow. Really
             shoulda warmed up first.

CHRISTINE: I can't wait to see the dancing Irish people with you.

JOEY: And I can't wait to go to Europe with you.

CHRISTINE: Me, too.

JOEY: Countdown, four months.

CHRISTINE: I know.

JOEY: Four...months!

CHRISTINE: I...know!

JOEY: Just think about it. We're finally gonna be, like, alone. A lot.

CHRISTINE: All the time.

JOEY: All the time!

CHRISTINE: Just you and me.

JOEY: Together.

CHRISTINE: Out in the open.

JOEY: Yeah. What do you mean?

CHRISTINE: I mean...freedom. Free to do whatever.

JOEY: *(hands on CHRISTINE's waist, eyebrow raised)* Whatever?

CHRISTINE: Don't ruin the moment, perv.

JOEY: You brought up the possibility of *whatever*...

CHRISTINE: Joey...

JOEY: Sorry, sorry. Guy moment. Shake it off. *(he shakes it off, beat)* And I'm back.

CHRISTINE: Tell me what you see. When you think of it. Us over there. Together.

JOEY: All right. I'll paint you the picture... Close your eyes. Close 'em up.

> CHRISTINE does. JOEY holds her...speaks softly into her ear...

JOEY: Me and you. You and me... Trudging across the rolling hills of Ireland... Cutting through the dark, magical forests of Scotland...

CHRISTINE: Paris. Don't forget Paris.

JOEY: Sitting outside a bakery in Gay Par-ee, sipping a fancy coffee and smelling the pastries…

CHRISTINE: I'm there.

JOEY: Sailing on the canals of Venice, moonlight reflecting in those gorgeous eyes of yours… Stuffin' our faces at every frickin' waffle factory in Belgium…!

Beat. CHRISTINE opens her eyes.

CHRISTINE: Belgium doesn't sound quite as romantic.

JOEY: You don't think waffles and romance go together?

CHRISTINE playfully elbows him in the stomach. He grabs for her playfully, she pulls away. Teasing.

JOEY: So I'm thinkin' we need to book our tickets. Better deal if we do it soon.

CHRISTINE: Mmm, hmm.

JOEY: What? What is it?

CHRISTINE: Nothing. Just. Little wrinkle at home. I'll deal with it.

JOEY: They're not letting you go.

CHRISTINE: It's not that.

JOEY: They know we're planning—?

CHRISTINE: Of course… But my dad. He's making noise about wanting to take us to China in the summer. See where he and Mom grew up. Might overlap into the fall a bit.

JOEY: Oh… Oh.

CHRISTINE: Stupid. Don't worry. I'm getting out of it.

JOEY: No, that might be cool.

CHRISTINE: Cool? You haven't met my parents.

JOEY: No I haven't. But, but think about it. What if we, like, combined the two? You and your folks do the China thing, maybe I fly out later, meet you there.

CHRISTINE: In China?

JOEY: In China, yeah.

CHRISTINE: What? Just meet you on a street corner?

JOEY: We'll figure it out.

CHRISTINE: I don't think—

JOEY: It's perfect. You get your family time, I get to know your folks, then we're on our way to Europe.

CHRISTINE: It's not like Europe's a day trip away from China, Joey. That... There'd be a lot of planning—

JOEY: I can do all that, I've been mucking around on the Net. It'd be awesome!

CHRISTINE: Yeah, but... I mean, who'd want to go to China?

JOEY: I dunno. I mean, there's like a trillion people there, right? Gotta be stuff to see. Oh, and they got that wall, eh?

CHRISTINE: Uh, huh.

JOEY: Big ol' wall. Hey, that's where we could meet up. "Meet ya at the big Chinese wall, Chris! Wednesday! Six-ish!" Although I'm a little worried about the food over there. Heard they like their dogs a little too much, in a way different way than we do. Like...snacking on—

CHRISTINE: I get it, Joey.

JOEY: Us together, right? Who cares where we go...as long as we go.

CHRISTINE: You'd really do that? For me?

JOEY: For us.

Beat. JOEY starts dribbling the basketball.

There's this Chinese guy who plays for Houston, right? Yao Ming? Giant. A living giant and apparently he's not alone. Doyle says there's this one special region in China where the dudes grow massive!

JOEY dribbles. Stands up on the bench. Passes the ball to CHRISTINE, shielding the "net"—garbage can—with his body.

JOEY: No one can get past him. Too big, too fast. Come on. Try.

CHRISTINE: What?

JOEY: Take a shot. Guy blocks everything, come on. Shoot.

> *CHRISTINE dribbles. Awkwardly. JOEY laughs.*

CHRISTINE: Shut up.

JOEY: Elbows up, sweetheart.

CHRISTINE: I know how to throw a ball, genius.

JOEY: Shoot, Chris. It's called shooting.

CHRISTINE: Fine.

> *CHRISTINE readies herself. Raises the ball, looking to shoot. JOEY gets his arms up, preparing to block... Then CHRISTINE calmly steps past JOEY on the bench and easily lays the ball into the can. She imitates JOEY's "buzzer" sound, mocks him, taunts him.*

CHRISTINE: Oh, yeah! I love this game!

JOEY: No way. You traveled.

CHRISTINE: In...the...face!

JOEY: In your face. The phrase is—

CHRISTINE: I schooled you, giant Chinese man.

JOEY: You so traveled. No basket.

CHRISTINE: *(looks off)* Ref? *(makes buzzer sound again)* Point to Christine!

> *JOEY hops off the bench, chases CHRISTINE down. Smothers her in his arms, holding her from behind.*

CHRISTINE: Foul! Foul! Yer foul!

JOEY: You are.

> *He kisses her. Nuzzles her neck. Holds her. Beat.*

JOEY: How come you don't see big Chinamen walking around here?

CHRISTINE: What?

JOEY: They're all small. Tiny. Step up from dwarfish. Why is that?

CHRISTINE: I don't—

JOEY: Is it like a genetic thing? Growth genes are like defective? Rice overdose?

> *Pause.* CHRISTINE *slowly, gently, releases herself from* JOEY.

CHRISTINE: I don't know.

JOEY: I'm just askin'.

CHRISTINE: Can we change the subject please?

JOEY: Why are you gettin' all—?

CHRISTINE: I'm not gettin' all anything, okay? This is…boring. Who cares about—? Forget it.

> *Pause.*

JOEY: I was just sayin'—

CHRISTINE: I know. You always…

JOEY: I always what? What'd I do?

> CHRISTINE *considers. Beat…*

CHRISTINE: Nothing. I'll get out of the China trip. It's fine.

JOEY: But I thought—

CHRISTINE: It's fine!

> *Pause.*

Sorry. I'm just…it's warm out here. I'm hot.

JOEY: No kiddin'!

CHRISTINE: I mean I need a Slurpee. My treat, let's go.

JOEY: Uh, okay.

> JOEY *starts off left.* CHRISTINE *follows, then stops.* JOEY *looks back.*

JOEY: C'mon. Mac's is this way.

CHRISTINE: *(pause)* Let's go to Chan's this time.

JOEY: Why? We never go there.

CHRISTINE: In the mood for change, I guess.

JOEY: But…Mac's has way better Slurpees, more selection.

CHRISTINE: It's farther away. I have to be home for dinner soon. Let's just go to Chan's.

JOEY: Actually, you know what? I don't feel like a Slurpee now.

CHRISTINE: You don't?

JOEY: Nah. I had like three Cokes at school today. No more sugar for me.

CHRISTINE: Uh, huh. *(beat)* You know, you're right. Mac's does have way better Slurpees. Let's go there.

JOEY: You sure?

CHRISTINE: Absolutely. It's worth the extra few blocks. Let's go.

JOEY: Yeah, okay.

CHRISTINE: But I thought you had too much sugar today. Changed your mind twice there in a matter of seconds.

JOEY: I meant I'd go along for the walk, I didn't change my mind.

CHRISTINE: Along for the walk?

JOEY: Yeah.

CHRISTINE: Okay. Walk with me to Chan's then.

JOEY: Fine.

CHRISTINE: Walk with me to Chan's, then when we get there, go inside with me.

> CHRISTINE *starts off right,* JOEY *lags behind, stops following.* CHRISTINE *stops, looks back at him. Beat.*

CHRISTINE: What would happen, Joey? If you walked into Mister Chan's store right now? Would he greet you happily? Ask how you've been?… Or would he go all quiet? Could he look you in the eye? Would he kick you out, call the cops, would—?

JOEY: All right.

CHRISTINE: All right what?

JOEY: I was in the store last night. But I had nothin' to do with—

CHRISTINE: That's two.

JOEY: Two what?

CHRISTINE: That is, at the very least, the second time I've caught you in a big lie this afternoon.

JOEY: It's not that big. I was—

CHRISTINE: I asked you repeatedly, a thousand times, were you in the store last night and you said no.

JOEY: Because I didn't want you to think…

CHRISTINE: What? That you're honest?

JOEY: I didn't want you to think badly of me or my brother before you heard all the facts! You weren't there, you don't know what—

CHRISTINE: So tell me.

JOEY: It wasn't as big a deal as—

CHRISTINE: So tell me what happened!

JOEY: Quit interruptin' me and I will!… Mister Chan short-changed Doyle. Okay? And he wouldn't admit he messed up… Look, I never had a problem with Mister Chan before, but he… he was wrong. Doyle just wanted the rest of his change and Chan got all…like, defensive. Told us to get out and…I mean, Doyle's got a bit of a short fuse but he didn't…

CHRISTINE: Struggling to get your facts straight? Or are you just making it up as you go along?

JOEY: Doyle didn't start it, all right?

CHRISTINE: Why should I believe you now?

JOEY: I've never lied to you before.

CHRISTINE: You mean except for those two earlier?

JOEY: "Those two"? Is this some game that I don't know the rules of? You keepin' score?

CHRISTINE: I am not playing around here!

JOEY: Why are you gettin' so worked up about this?

CHRISTINE: Nasty, disgusting words were flung at Mister Chan last night. Why do you think I'm worked up?

JOEY: I dunno.

CHRISTINE: Mister Chan is Chinese.

JOEY: Yeah, and?

CHRISTINE: Look at me, Joey. And brace yourself… I'm Chinese!

JOEY: I know that.

CHRISTINE: Then how do you think I feel hearing that my boyfriend's brother was hurling racial slurs at a Chinese man?

JOEY: I didn't! And besides, you're not really Chinese.

          Pause. CHRISTINE *just stares, incredulous.*

JOEY: I mean, don't take it the wrong way or anything.

          Pause. She just stares.

JOEY: See, I think you're taking it the wrong way.

CHRISTINE: How…on earth…should I take it?

JOEY: You should take it well.

CHRISTINE: I'm not Chinese, you say?

JOEY: Not like Mister Chan is.

CHRISTINE: Oh my god.

JOEY: What I mean is—

CHRISTINE: No, no. I get it. I don't own a convenience store so I'm not really Chinese, that it?

JOEY: No, I—

CHRISTINE: I don't carry around fortune cookies in my pocket or talk with a "wewy wewy tick" accent so I'm not Chinese?

JOEY: I never said that.

CHRISTINE: I didn't spend sixty days in the hull of some oil tanker, smuggled into the country so I'm not really—

JOEY: Would you let me clarify here? You're blowing this out of… You just don't look or act all that, you know…ethnic. *(pause)* I'm not sayin' it like it's a bad thing or…

CHRISTINE just stares at him. Stunned.

JOEY: What? Why are you looking at me like that?

CHRISTINE: Six months. For six months I said nothing… Started small. Little things, but I kept ignoring them.

JOEY: What are you on about now?

CHRISTINE: On our second date we went for dinner at Pappa Pasta and our waiter was Chinese. You asked him for the free bread, he said they were out, and after he took our order and walked away you said "He better not put sweet n' sour on my fettuccine."

JOEY: I don't remember that.

CHRISTINE: We were Christmas shopping in that dollar store, you thought the Arabic man behind the counter was "eyeing" you, watching your every move, so on your way out you make some muttered dig about how he should never be allowed on an airplane.

JOEY: Come on, Chris, that was a joke. It had nothing—

CHRISTINE: "East Indians are cheap," "Duck down! That Asian gang's packin' heat!", "Why you grow so small? Rice overdose?"—

JOEY: Oh, gimme a break. Are you—?

CHRISTINE: It never, NEVER occurred to you that any of that stuff might be hurtful to me?

JOEY: It had nothin' to do with you.

CHRISTINE: Because I'm not really "ethnic."

JOEY: No. I don't think of you as like that. I think of you as a girl, a girl I like, that's it. Geez, Chris, they were just jokes. Words.

CHRISTINE: So words can't hurt? Jokes can't hurt?

JOEY: Hey. I take as much ribbing as the next—

CHRISTINE: Oh, please.

JOEY: I do! Make a joke about my pointy head again! I love it, it's awesome!

CHRISTINE: That's not the same thing!… All this time. I never wanted to believe. He's cute, he's nice to me, so who cares if he's a…

JOEY: What? *(no response)* No, I think you're gonna finish that sentence! I'm what?… *(beat, eyes widen)* Oh, man… My own girlfriend thinks I'm a racist? How can you think that about me? All this time us bein' together and now all of a sudden you…

CHRISTINE: I don't think it's your fault. Entirely.

JOEY: · Oh…of course… My brother is the king of all racists and I'm just following in his footsteps. That it?

CHRISTINE: You need to wake up to the fact that your hero brother does not like minorities.

JOEY: You don't know a thing about my brother.

CHRISTINE: I know he doesn't like me.

JOEY: Bull.

CHRISTINE: How many times have I been to your house?

JOEY: A few times.

CHRISTINE: Family dinner, three months ago. One time only.

JOEY: But I invited you way more than that.

CHRISTINE: And I only went once. Why do you think that is?

JOEY: Why don't you tell me? You've got all the answers.

CHRISTINE: Because from the moment I stepped in your house I knew Doyle was disgusted that his younger brother was dating a chink.

          Silence.

JOEY: Look, you want to label me a racist, fine. But I ain't gonna let you disrespect my family. We know enough about discrimination and bein' repressed an' all—

CHRISTINE: Oh, here we go.

JOEY: Here we go what?

CHRISTINE: Here comes the cloverleaf power speech.

JOEY: Hey, I'm proud to be Irish.

CHRISTINE: That's super, Joey, but you're, like, what? An eighth Irish? You're also German, Scot, little Dutch, what else?

JOEY: What's your point?

CHRISTINE: Buying tickets to some stupid Dancing River show, eating Lucky Charms, and watching Celtics games with your alcoholic dad doesn't make you pure Irish!

JOEY: *(pause)* Well, well. Everyone hear that?

CHRISTINE: I… I didn't mean that, it was—

JOEY: What? Just words? A joke? About *my* father? You don't even know him!

CHRISTINE: You're right. And I'm sorry.

JOEY: I'm a racist? Fine. So are you.

CHRISTINE: That's not the same thing. You're not completely Irish, I'm entirely Chinese.

JOEY: Where were you born?

CHRISTINE: What does that—?

JOEY: Answer me. Where were you born?

CHRISTINE: Here.

JOEY: Me, too.

CHRISTINE: So?

JOEY: So cut this you're pure and I'm mixed crap. We're the same.

CHRISTINE: You honestly, *honestly* think we're the same?

JOEY: Yeah.

CHRISTINE: Really?

JOEY: Yes!

CHRISTINE: Look at my eyes. Look at my skin… Now do you think
             we're the same?

JOEY: It's not about—

CHRISTINE: Ever get called "yellow"? Huh? People walk down the street
             and do this to you? *(pushes her eyes slanted…sings)* "Me
             Chinese, me so dumb, me play knick-knack on my—"

JOEY: All right. You made your point.

CHRISTINE: Then don't EVER say we're the same. I don't care that we
             were born in the same country, look in a mirror! You don't
             know a thing about bearing the brunt of racist comments.
             About what it feels like to have hatred shooting out of
             people's eyes at you. Like I felt at your house that time.

JOEY: Well at least you were invited to my house.

CHRISTINE: You've been in my house before.

JOEY: Yeah. After school only, when your folks are at work, and
             I'm always mysteriously shoved out the door just after the
             five o'clock whistle blows.

CHRISTINE: You're changing the subject. I want to know—

JOEY: How come I've never met your parents? I mean, do they
             even know about me?

CHRISTINE: Of course they do.

JOEY: What do they know about me?

CHRISTINE: That we're friends and—

JOEY: Friends.

CHRISTINE: They know I spend time with you.

JOEY: Why is it then that every time I pick you up you're waiting
             on the front doorstep? Even in the middle of winter, I pull
             up and you're right there waiting. Outside… You ashamed
             of me?

CHRISTINE: No.

JOEY: Sure of that?

CHRISTINE: Don't be ridic—

JOEY: Okay, then. Let's go to your place, right now. Wait till dinner time, your parents walk in the front door…and you can introduce me to them.

CHRISTINE: Don't turn this around on me, you're the one who—

JOEY: I'll shake their hands, put my arm around you and give you a big, fat ten-minute kiss right in front of them. Sound good? Your folks gathered round while their daughter swaps spit with a white boy. Let's go do that, right this second. Then we'll see—

CHRISTINE: Okay!

JOEY: Okay what?

CHRISTINE: My parents don't know you're my boyfriend! And you're white!

JOEY: That's one.

CHRISTINE: What?

JOEY: Actually that's two. We're all tied up, folks.

CHRISTINE: That's not the… I lied to my parents, you lied to *me*.

JOEY: Referee's ruling? *(looks off—buzzer noise)* Same difference. Two points to Big J.

CHRISTINE: What are you—?

JOEY: I started slow, but since half-time I've been runnin' you up and down the—

CHRISTINE: This is not a game, Joey!

JOEY: Your defence? Weak. Exposed. Oh sure you're good on the offence, with the unfounded accusations, but get pushed back a bit and suddenly you have no answer for what I'm bringin'!

CHRISTINE: I'm not ashamed of you, okay?

JOEY: Then what?

CHRISTINE: It's me.

JOEY: You're ashamed of yourself?

CHRISTINE: No! I… Look, you don't know my parents. They're old school Chinese, traditional, protective…

JOEY: What's the worst that would happen? If they knew about us? They want you to only date Chinese guys?

CHRISTINE: They don't want me to date, period.

JOEY: You're seventeen!

CHRISTINE: You don't understand.

JOEY: But if they did let you date?

CHRISTINE: Then, yes. Yes! Slant-eyed brown dwarfs only need apply!

JOEY: I see… But my *brother* is the racist…

CHRISTINE: They want what's best—to protect—it's a cultural—

JOEY: My family may not be entirely thrilled I'm dating a Chinese girl…

CHRISTINE: So you admit it.

JOEY: …But at least they KNOW I'm dating a Chinese girl! I've never hid that from them. And they've never said anything or tried to stop me. And obviously their opinions wouldn't matter to me anyway because I'm still with you. I don't care what anyone says or thinks about us. Unlike you. You're the one who's petrified of what your family might think! You're the one who's scared to death of anyone seeing who you really are!

CHRISTINE: You want to know who I really am, Joey?

JOEY: That'd be nice, yeah.

CHRISTINE: I'm Mister Chan's niece!

               Long silence.

JOEY: He's your uncle?

CHRISTINE: My mom's brother.

JOEY: You never told—

CHRISTINE: No, I didn't. Didn't tell anyone.

JOEY: Why?

CHRISTINE: Because that's what I'm ashamed of! Because if I'm related to the typical, pathetic old Chinese convenience store owner, then I'm one of "them." And that's how you'd always see me.

JOEY: That's not true.

CHRISTINE: In my home, you don't exist. And at school I don't exist! I spend every waking second trying not to stand out!

JOEY: Why would you do that?

CHRISTINE: Because if I don't, any jerk-off could treat me the same way your brother treated Mist— My uncle! My family!

JOEY: *(beat, stunned)* Your…your family was disrespected, I…

CHRISTINE: My cousin, Mindy, was in the back. Heard voices. Didn't look out but swore she heard you.

JOEY: I—

CHRISTINE: But I defended you. Not Joey, no. Had to be his brother. Joey would never…

JOEY: If I'd known he was your uncle—

CHRISTINE: If you stood by and did nothing while your brother—

JOEY: It's not—

CHRISTINE: —I'll forgive you.

JOEY: You will?

CHRISTINE: I just want the truth. If we deal with the truth, we'll…we'll be okay. No more lying, either of us.

JOEY: I don't want to lie to you again.

CHRISTINE: Then you have to stop defending him. This wasn't the first time. He had run-ins with my uncle, my aunt, many times. Why do you think it was so hard for me to be around him at your house?

JOEY: Doyle…didn't do anything last night.

CHRISTINE: You already told me—

JOEY: He tried to break it up.

CHRISTINE: So… So it was his friend Shane who said those things?

JOEY: No.

> *Pause.*

> We walk in. Three of us. Bag of chips, three Slurpees. Total came up as seven dollars, fifty-six cents. Doyle hands him a twenty. Mister Chan gives him back two dollars and forty-four cents. Doyle says I gave you a twenty. "No. You gave me ten…" Neither one budging… All these years, goin' in to his shop…he never knew… He looks me right in the eye and says "I never knew this jerk was your brother." I wipe the counter clean, grab him by the collar and said, "Yeah? Well I never knew you were one a' them cheap, ignorant, short-changin', smelly chinks." I pushed him, hard, he crashed into the wall. Doyle tried to calm things down, almost had me outside…but I went back, grabbed his little candy dish off the counter, smashed it on the ground and said, "Sorry about that. Looks like I broke your rice bowl." Then we go.

> *Pause.*

> And it wasn't 'cause he was Chinese, Chris, you have to understand that. That's got nothin' to do with… He disrespected me, my family. You get that, right?… Right?… What was I supposed to do!

> *Silence.*

> Say something.

> *Silence.*

> Please. Say something.

> *Silence.*

> Get mad, scream. You have every right. *(beat, moves to her)* I'm sorry.

CHRISTINE: Don't.

JOEY: I could have kept lying, but I didn't. I gave you what you wanted, I gave you the truth and you said we would be okay. *(beat)* We can get through this. Keep being honest, help each other.

Silence.

Look, I know we've had like a tense day here, you know, lotsa crazy stuff said but… Christine, please. Please. I will make this up to you. And to your uncle, I will apologize to him over and over again. I will. And I won't lie to you again, I swear, just…please don't give up on me. On us.

CHRISTINE turns to leave. As she's almost gone…

JOEY: Christine, I love you.

CHRISTINE stops. Pause. Slowly turns around.

JOEY: You want truth? There. I love you so much.

CHRISTINE slowly moves back. Close to JOEY. Looks at him.

CHRISTINE: Truth? *(JOEY nods)* I don't know.

CHRISTINE walks off. JOEY stands, stunned, watching her walk away. He slowly walks back to the bench, sits down, head between his legs, running his hands through his hair. He exhales a large breath. He picks up his basketball, gets up. Starts dribbling, talking to himself. Looking to the hoop.

JOEY: See, at this point he knows… He knows…

JOEY aims his shot. Holds it. Stops. Slowly lowers the ball.

He's got no shot.

JOEY sets the ball down on the ground. Exits.

Lights down.

The End

Recent Production History

2009 — Quest Theatre, Calgary
Director   Duval Lang
Joey   Phil Fulton
Christine   Denise Wong

2008 — Theatre Direct, Toronto
Director   Andrea Donaldson
Joey   Colin Doyle
Christine   Ella Chan

Received two Dora Nominations for Outstanding Production and Outstanding Performance (Ensemble), Young Audiences Division.

2006 — Concrete Theatre, Edmonton
Director   Jared Matsunaga-Turnbull
Joey   Chris Bullough
Christine   Nadien Chu

1999-2000 — All Nations Theatre Society, Calgary
Director   Natasha Nadir
Joey   David Beazely
Christine   Karen Chin

Acknowledgements

Offensive Fouls was originally commissioned and produced in Calgary, Alberta by All Nations International Theatre Society (Natasha Nadir, former Artistic Director) in 1999-2000. The playwright wishes to thank Natasha and the cast of the initial production for their invaluable contributions.

The playwright also wishes to acknowledge and thank Jared Matsunaga-Turnbull and Concrete Theatre in Edmonton, Alberta for their assistance in workshopping and reshaping the play in the summer/fall of 2006.

About the Playwright

Jason Long is busy working on two new plays for young audiences: *In The Club*, commissioned by Quest Theatre of Calgary, and *The Daily Mischief: Haunted Summer* for Calgary Young People's Theatre (a sequel to *The Daily Mischief*). His most recognized play for young audiences, *Offensive Fouls*, has toured across Canada in productions by several well respected TYA companies, including Theatre Direct in Toronto, whose production garnered two Dora nominations in 2008. Jason has also co-written two feature film screenplays, *Turning Paige* and *Walk All Over Me*. He also teaches screenwriting and playwriting for adults and youth, and is a graduate of The National Theatre School Of Canada.

Interview

I can reflect back now and say that writing for young audiences was/ is the place where my words and ideas make the most sense. But as for that first initial "gig," this play *Offensive Fouls* was my first true foray into writing for young audiences.

I was fresh out of the National Theatre School, back home in Calgary, and my good friend Natasha Nadir was at the helm of a small but ambitious TYA company named *All Nations Theatre.* She was looking to commission a one-act touring play on racism, and I piped up without really listening to the words coming out of my mouth (as I am prone to do): "How racist does it need to be??"

I had been kicking around some dialogue about two young teens, male and female, meeting on a deserted schoolyard basketball court. And really, it was pretty vanilla. Rambling, sarcastic, no form to it. I was hoping that by just getting them talking, magic would transpire and a story would unfold. No. Just a couple of young cynical teens shooting the breeze. And hoops.

But this lame scene, plus Natasha's hunt for a play about racism, equaled my first real shot at a commission. So I altered "the girl" to Christine, of Asian descent, and was off and running. The backstories and character histories seemed, in retrospect, readily available to me and I don't recall stretches of ever truly being blocked in the creation of this play — which I bring up only to point out how supremely rare this is for me. Did not happen before, has not happened since!

Writing for young audiences as opposed to adults has many insignificant differences, but only one that truly matters to me from the writing perspective: young audiences, in schools, traditionally have no choice. School buys the show, school makes them sit in the gym or auditorium. For some students this could be a welcome break from math or science; for others, they are walking in, eyes rolling and ready to rip on your work, so you better bring something that grabs them. Adults can buy their tickets to an A house, see a play, and walk away going "How terrible was that?" yet know that on some level, they chose. They bought the ticket, they made the call. So for me, writing work for young audiences that I hope will make it into schools, I feel an extra sense of importance in bringing challenging, surprising, and *entertaining* stories that go well beyond the commissioned theme or subject matter.

The initial development was very smooth between Natasha Nadir and me. I was a fledgling writer, they a fledgling company, and because Natasha and I had a previous working relationship and solid friendship, there were no egos involved. It was a very tight timeline, knocking off two to three drafts in five months time to get it rehearsal ready, so there was not a lot of time to reflect and let new ideas soak in. From inception to first tour, less than six months, which seems crazy, but I remember once the show was up and running thinking to myself, "It's done... I have *finally* finished a play. No more rewrites!"

All Nations did another very, very small tour a year later, Geordie Productions of Montreal did an extensive tour in 2003-04, and then it sat. And sat. And scripts got sent out...and no replies came back.

Then I received a phone call out of the blue from Jared Matsunaga-Turnbull, an Artistic Associate of Concrete Theatre in Edmonton. I had seen Jared act before and you don't quite forget a handle like his. He cut right to the chase: Likes the play, wants me to rewrite it. (The voice, in my head, from waaaay back when: "It's done... No more rewrites!" ...But then, just as quickly, my "other" voice countered, "But no one has even shown an interest in producing it in years!") So I said YES, PLEASE.

Jared brought me up to Edmonton for a weekend, we read, we workshopped, we talked. And we laughed A LOT. The play as it was, and the play Jared wanted, had one key difference between them. In his words, the play as it was then, "Reads like a commission." This was indeed true. Great patter, pace and tone for two-thirds of the piece, and then...bring on the speeches. Racism is bad. Don't be racist...and the drama, the stakes, the high tension...were lost. Read it as fast and with as much emotion as possible...it didn't matter. It died every time.

"It's a love story," Jared said to me bluntly. "Write it like a love story." I could almost feel the shackles come off and THUD to the floor! "I can do that?" That night in my hotel room I did the most significant reworking of the play I had done in years, and by the next day felt that I had the best of both worlds. Same story, same characters, *way better play.* It's safe to say this piece would not have received future productions/tours had Jared not taken the time to bring me up to Edmonton and allow me to write the story as it needed to be written.

Offensive Fouls unfolds in real time. In writing the first draft I don't recall ever consciously making that choice. George F. Walker's *Tough!* was a revelatory read for me, as I'm sure it was/is for many playwrights, so I have no doubt that the choices he made in writing that seminal piece of TYA influenced me greatly.

I'm a huge fan of plays, for all audiences, that use the real time structure. If properly executed, it does not give the audience a moment to breathe, or check in with themselves or deconstruct what they've just witnessed. From the start, it's one big push to the climax. They just don't know it yet. There's the voyeuristic quality that has appeal as well. Like we are peeking in on 45 crucial minutes in the lives of two young people. I'm fascinated by the great lengths to which people go to sustain lies, or to fracture and manipulate truth when it suits them most.

As for feedback from past productions? My favorite feedback—*of all time*—below. This is what one young student had to say in a blog, after seeing Theatre Direct's production at her school:

"So, last Thursday, my class was invited to see a play performed at our school called *Offensive Fouls.* I was tempted to skip because I had assignments that were unfinished that I had to hand in two periods later, and watching these plays always seemed like a waste of time, because they were usually dull and preachy, and I couldn't recall a single moment in my life when I watched a play performed in school that I actually liked... However! I am actually glad I stayed. The play was excellent... It wasn't preachy in the slightest. It took on the questioning approach, throwing questions that didn't have a defined right or wrong answer to them at the audience, and withholding the answers so that the audience can come up with their own thoughts... Playing the story this way stops us from placing judgment on the characters, and simply allows us to see them as real teenagers with real teenager relationship problems..."

This young person is who I try to write for. Every day. And I can't thank her enough.

Learning The Game

by Janice Salkeld

Characters

LANNI — a feminine, athletic 15-year-old. She also plays the characters of the teachers Ms. W, MR. RAZNIK, Ms. M., BEIGE BETH, Ms. NORSDALE, MR. PETERS, and the OPPOSITION HOCKEY PLAYER.

Setting

A locker room with a bench and some equipment. She is her own audience.

LANNI, a very physical young girl, enters with a hockey bag in hand. Through the play she eventually starts preparing for a game. She may do warm-ups, put skate laces in, perhaps put roller blades on to do a few laps, tape her stick, etc. She should be in full hockey gear by the end. She should use hockey tape — both stick and sock tape — to make a hockey tape "ball." It should be large enough by the end that she can shoot it.) When she enters she is singing the Happy Birthday song to Mr. Peters — may repeat or sing as much of it as necessary, as long as we hear his name. [Note this same birthday song is picked up again at a later juncture in the play.] She is extremely angry, and works at calming herself down. The coach she refers to throughout the play is her hockey coach, Coach Boone, and not her volleyball coach, Mr. Peters.

LANNI: *(sings angrily)* Happy Birthday, Mr. Peters. Happy Birthday to you. *(Pause. She kicks over the garbage can)* No, Coach Boone. You're right. It doesn't sound like any happy birthday song you've ever heard sung. But you've never heard anyone sing it when they're this angry.

Yeah, yeah. I know what you tell me. C'mon, Lanni. Get it under control. Angry players make dumb mistakes. How can you play from a position of strength? What do you know? Well, let's see. Name's Lanni. Ordinary looking girl. Some people still look at me and assume this is my boyfriend's or my brother's hockey bag. But it isn't. It's mine. Yep. Time to rethink things, isn't it? First thought that shoots through your mind? She sure don't look like no hockey player. Second thought? Wonder if she's a lesbian. Third thought — what's she trying to prove? Fourth thought — oh, get real. You might be bright, but you haven't had time for that many thoughts yet!

Now you're thinking…she's a little feminine to be a hockey player. They're supposed to be big and bulky and butch. Wonder what position she plays? Wonder if she's any good? *(flexes)* Just look at these pipes. Go ahead. Look. Wanna feel one? Yeah. That's right. Nice and muscular. I work hard at it. I work hard at everything. *(whips down, does crunches)* 201, 202, 203, 204, 205. Sorry, but when you're trying to do 400 of these in a day, you have to use whatever time you've got. That's right. I said 400. Now my differences are starting to show, aren't they? The good kind of differences.

Being scouted. Being picked up by a team. The thrill is huge! Little tricky, though. *(she takes a skate and tries to put it on)* Having that 6th toe to fit into the skate without anyone noticing. I don't want to draw attention to myself. I don't want to be different. I just want to fit in. I mean, what if you have to have specially made skates? Man, nobody does that in girl's hockey. That's strictly for figure skaters. *(music such as "The Skater's Waltz," she mimes a figure skater getting hit by a hard check. Boarding sound)* And if you have a whiff of figure skating about you in a hockey game, you're dead meat on the ice. *(stands as though she's looking over top of someone)* Almost as bad as saying you actually like ringette. Dude. I'm pulling your leg now. *(pause)* At least about the 6th toe. But the part about it being tricky — that's for real. See, if I had something like a 6th toe…that'd be totally okay. But you want to try a learning disability on for size. It fits too tight and that smarts…if you'll forgive the pun.

You look skeptical. I know what everybody thinks. First thought — she doesn't look like she has a learning disability. Second thought — she doesn't sound like she has a learning disability. Third thought — wait a minute, her self-esteem seems pretty intact. Fourth thought — c'mon. I might have a learning disability, but even I know you haven't had time for a fourth thought yet.

Yeah, Coach. Joking around. That's one of the ways I get through a tough spot. Look, I've been joking around, right? Up here *(indicates head)* the words still come out. But here… *(indicates heart)* C'mon. Skate backward with me to the beginning, and I'll tell you about it from how I've seen things. I've coped. You'll see.

So. Kindergarten was fun. But I always wondered if between then and grade one everybody else got special information in their dreams or studied special books I didn't know about, because in grade one it was different. Things got hard for me, but my friends seemed to do okay. I just wanted to run home where it was safe. I was — confused. Gym class was the same as kindergarten. I could climb higher, run further and throw the ball harder than everybody else, even the boys. But outside of gym class, I had to sit in a desk. Colours were easy, and stories were great, but the rest of it... By grade 4 it was harder to do the work. When I did homework with my teammates, they said it was easy. They always finished way before me, so I quit working with them. I didn't want them to think I was stupid or something. I needed to be smart enough to know how to deke around the stuff that I couldn't do. Just like hockey. *(she demos — may use a stick and a hockey ball or roller puck for this. She can bounce it on the flat of the blade, too. Sound of puck on stick, and of shots.)* Bank shot, wrist shot. If you have trouble with it one way, try another. Slapshot, back hand.

One day Ms. W. gave us a big photocopied social studies assignment full of charts and maps. It was long and tedious, like some hockey drills. But I worked hard and finished it. On time, too. I was so proud of it that I signed my name with a big flourish. I felt good, and when I handed it in, I was smiling.

Ms. W: What is this? There's even a spelling error in the first line. Why are you standing there smirking?

Lanni: I didn't mean to smirk. I thought I was smiling. Sometimes she makes me so nervous and confused I can't even think.

Ms. W: You don't take anything seriously, young lady. This work is a disgrace. It isn't done. *(she rips up the paper and lets the pieces fall)* And you aren't trying nearly hard enough. *(we hear a whistle blow three times)*

Lanni: No goal, ladies and gentlemen, the ref just waved it off. My paper. All that work. I was... I took the pieces home, and that night, when nobody could see, I cried. But I'm not a whiny crier, am I, Coach? So instead I got mad. I chucked my ball of hockey tape around as hard as I could. When I got tired, I sat down and stared at all those pieces of paper, and started moving them around. When you lose a game, sometimes it isn't because you didn't try hard enough. You have a look at your game plan and try to analyze it. That gave me an idea. I taped the page back together again. But I still didn't know what was so wrong that I got a major penalty. I figured I needed a coach to help me out. I went to see my older brother, Dennis. He edited it, and I rewrote it again. Then I decided to protect my position. I taped the whole page until it was shiny and strong. The next day, I handed the teacher that carefully taped page. She may not have liked it, but she knew this one was too tough to shred. Since she couldn't write on that shiny sheet, she'd taped a little piece of paper to the bottom with her comments — some were even good.

By grade 6, I had a smart mouth and I was athletic, so I was a class leader, but my school work was tanking.

The teachers didn't notice me as much if I was the first one to volunteer to move benches in the gym, or get everybody outside at recess when it was really cold. Well, dude, it's better than sitting inside playing a stupid game like hangman. But my parents noticed how much homework I had. I couldn't distract them like I did the teacher. If I volunteered to help around the house the way I did at school it made them think I was up to something. They decided something had to be done, but geez, you don't want your parents messing around in your school stuff, except to show up at the right time and try to act like all the other parents, right? But nothing I could say changed their minds. As soon as my parents talked to the teacher she agreed something seemed a little "wonky" and "we" could probably use some extra help. *(she plays)*

It's like I'm playing in this major game. The score is tied, and the play is zinging from one end of the ice to the other. I call on every ounce of strength I have. Sweat drips from my brow. There's a scrimmage for the puck, but I'm off to the side, just out of the play. Gasping for air, I wheel and spin, skating in just as the whistle blows. *(sound of hockey whistle)* The ref makes the call *(makes the motion for the roughing penalty, which is one punching motion to the side with the arm extending from the shoulder. She mouths as we hear the loudspeaker announce: "Two minutes for roughing to number 23.)* Hey! That's my number. What? No way! I wasn't doing anything wrong. But the call's been made. No point arguing. I skate to the penalty box, head down. I'm going to sit there for two whole minutes — helpless — hoping nothing bad happens to the team while I'm in there. The request for assessments was put in about late fall. It got responded to about *(we hear Christmas music, then Easter music, then "Take Me Out to the Ball Game")* the first week of June... So! We were just about to start when the tester realizes *(sound of school bell ringing, then Lanni in a flustered voice)"Oh my gosh, it's June!"* Get this. One of the things they were testing me for was to see if I knew about minutes, hours, days of the week and months of the year. But somehow, it had totally slipped their minds that it was JUNE! They were running out of time and they had year-end reports to write. They'd have to put the rest of my testing on hold until fall. As for me? I was hoping they'd just lose the whole thing in a pile of obscure file folders. Shhhhh.

Over summer we moved to a bigger, better house. I was in the same hockey zone, so my coach and teammates stayed the same, but I had to go to a new school. Yeah. Great. A new square box with new kids, new teachers, and new rules. Oh yayee. My new teachers draw their own conclusions about me.

MR. R: Why aren't you working on your math assignment?

LANNI: Gee, Mr. Raznik, *(she whips out a roll of hockey tape)* want to borrow some sock tape? I see yours are kind of baggy. *(does a high five, acts as if someone has grabbed the roll of hockey tape and is pulling her along.)* Hey! Back off. I always do it at home where I can concentrate, o.k.?

Ms. M: Lanni, where's your geography?

LANNI: Gee, geography. How far away was your camping trip this weekend? Any sandy beaches at that lake? That's great. *(does another high five)* Later, my lady.

Ms. M: Not later, now.

Lanni: What do you mean, not later? Handing things in on time is highly overrated. She didn't smile, so I explained that I was working on it at home. The teachers at my old school knew it was true, but somehow she interprets this as a smart alec comment, no matter how much I protest.

Ms. M: March. *(irate)* Let's go. Now.

Lanni: What do you mean, march? *(She gets marched along. She turns, brushing herself off in indignation)* Sheesh.

Yeah, dude, my new school pretty much sucks. My music teacher doesn't care that I can play piano by ear and keep a beat. *(She hums dun, dun, dun, dun like the build of the organ music heard at hockey games. She raps the next lines.)*

> She's upset 'cause I can't read music
> 'cause I sit with the guys
> at the back of the class
> not those precious girls up front.
> But,
> It's the guys I play
> Football with at noon an'
> mini-sticks at breaks
> so what the hey. *(end rap)*

My music mark drops faster than a puck at the face off. My homeroom teacher, Mr. Raznik, has basically decided I'm sassy and lazy. *(She grabs a book from the bag, lies on her back, reads. Pretends to see MR. RAZNIK.)*

I'm reading. Honest. What's wrong with lying like this to read?

Mr. R: For you, probably nothing. Lying on your back is likely how you'll end up spending most of your time anyway.

Lanni: What? *(beat)* I couldn't believe he'd said that. I felt like crying, or screaming at him. But I never swore at him or ratted him out. I just focused on what I'd learned in hockey. Take care of yourself. Patience with the puck.

Right, Coach? I watched that teacher like you watch the goalie. Glove side or stick side? Down low or up high? Look for their weakness, and then shoot for it. One day when the math class is misbehaving, Mr. Raznik tries a new approach.

MR. R: *(she portrays a large teacher)* The whole class can have extra recess time if one of you does something really well.

LANNI: I know he means something in math, but I say, "How about 50 crunches, Mr. Raznik?

MR. R: If you can count that high.

LANNI: He'd like to shut me down at 50, but my classmates really get into it, *(voices 97, 98, 99, 100)*. Want to match me for the next 100, Mr. Raznik?

MR. R: *(sound of kids laughing)* Hrmph. Class dismissed for an extra 15 minutes of recess.

LANNI: Ooh yeah. Score one for the dumb kid. One day soon after that I got called to the office. *(sound effect of kids saying "Oooh")* There's a few snickers and I'm wracking my brains wondering what my latest offense was. Pick A if you think I've run in the hall today. Pick B if you figure I had a verbal battle with one of the girls, and it's all about their hurt feelings and damaged egos. Pick C if you think Mr. Raznik has caught on to me erasing my name from the blackboard list of kids who're supposed to stay in after school. I strut out of the room feeling pretty confident that I can handle whatever it is. I've been dealing with this stuff since I was in grade one. Turns out it's D. None of the above. They're going to test me. Test my brain. Here it is all over again. Did I really think things were just going to get better?

I realize I must have shot right to the top of the wait list. Have my teachers been talking about me? I know it's likely because of my "attitude" in this new school. And some of the "imbalances" in my marks, too. But dude, what'm I supposed to do about that? Besides, everybody gets bad grades sometimes. That's just...pah...normal.

Beige Lady met me in the office, with the principal, Ms. Norsdale, looking on. Beige hair, beige suit, cream blouse — wow! Now there was a contrast for you. She had beige lipstick, too. Anyway, she smiled, and introduced herself.

> *Plays BETH. She has some obvious mannerism— perhaps pursing her lips, or sucking her cheeks in and out.*

BETH: How do you do. I'm Beth Borgstrom. *(pause)* Aren't you going to introduce yourself?"

LANNI: Nah. You paged me, so I figure you already know who I am. The right corner of the principal's lip twitched a bit.

BETH: Yes. Well. Your teachers have requested that we do some testing with you, and we have parental consent. It'll be fun.

LANNI: This time there was no beige smile, so I just stared at her.

BETH: *(walks primly)* Please follow me this way.

LANNI: I did *(imitates her)* and I caught one more twitch of the principal's mouth as I left. That was the last fun thing of that day, I can tell you. We went down into a little room that wasn't much bigger than a penalty box. *(cage light)*

BETH: Your full name? Parents' names? Grade? Previous school?

LANNI: It took about 2 seconds for the fidgets to set in. Man, what's the point of their records if they don't believe their own stuff? She gave me some multiple choice tests with these little bubble sheets to fill in. You know the drill — math, sentence structure. Whatever. I'd get tired and frustrated and bored. Time for a change, right, Coach? So *(she does the following)* I'd break the tip of the special HB pencil they give you. Then I'd grab a marker, and start marking really fast. *(she sings speedy music, "The Lone Ranger," da dun, da dun, da dun dun dun)*

BETH: You. You used felt marker. You ruined the answer sheet. Oh, my. I don't know if we should start over... Or...well, perhaps I'd better just...

LANNI: *(laughs)* See? Actually, that little room would get really stuffy, so when I was laughing my hardest, I'd... *(sputters and coughs)*

BETH: Oh, my. Goodness, let's just open the door, shall we?

LANNI: Once the door was open, *(repeat "Lone Ranger" music)* I'd take off. Sometimes I'd get all the way to the water fountain before getting called back. *(she laughs, enjoying it)*

I could tell Beige Lady was puzzled. Some stuff I tore through like a star defense breaking out and tearing down the ice on a rush, and burying it top corner. *(in an ANNOUNCER's voice)* It's a goal! Score one test for the dumb kid. But the next one *(referee's whistle blows)* — man, it's like the ref has just unfairly penalized my team.

Question: The top of the roof on the inside of a building is called a... That's easy, ceiling...spelled... *(spells out letters)* S E L L I N G, no, spelled S E E L I N G, no... Penalty. We're down two players. My body burns, but try as I might I can't stick handle that puck anywhere.

Question: 5+3-2+2 is... Does a plus or a minus cancel, or is that two questions? Did I skip a line? A normal shift on the ice is 40 or 50 seconds, but I've been on for two whole minutes. My lungs are on fire, my legs are numb, and my brain is shutting down. I let go a weak shot and miss the net. I need to try again.

BETH: Time.

LANNI: Not even a single shot on goal.

BETH: Time is up, Lanni.

LANNI: She looks serious. Concerned. I've seen that look before. It's quiet. Like in the dressing room after you just lost a game. You can't look at anyone or say anything. You tried...you tried so hard...you... *(through this she collapses)* Why? Why can't I just do stuff like everyone else? Why does it have to be so hard? If I'd eaten my peas like my brother, would it have fixed me? Why won't my brain work better? I want...I want my mummy, and a story, and for everything to be okay again. *(long pause)*

I finally get back to my regular classroom two days later. Yeah! Two days. Can you believe it? Hey, Thomas, wanna trade hockey cards at recess? Jenny, be my art partner? But nobody would look at me.

A meeting was finally called when I'd nearly forgotten about it, only it doesn't go away, does it?

My parents gave me the pre-game pep talk about how this meeting will give us some answers, and help find solutions. They tell me how smart I am, and how much they believe in me. You know the kind of loving parental jazz talk I mean. Hey, dude. Don't mean no disrespect to the Mum and the Dad. I count them as some of the best coaches…the good, positive, flag-waving, "you can do it" kind that you need.

BETH: We don't know why… Math and spelling scores are well below grade level, reading scores are grade 11 level — other scores except geography tend to be age/grade appropriate given norms for—

LANNI: Man, it took them two days of testing just to tell us what we already knew, except with a lot of big words… *(soft, restrained classical music such as Pachelbel's Canon)*

BETH: Although articulation strengths, possible overall temporal spatial disorganization, although her athletic ability counter indicates—

LANNI: I tune out and sit there quietly, dreaming up a new play for hockey, like I do in math class when I've stopped paying attention. *(we hear earlier soft music)*

BETH: You are to be commended for assisting in her superior coping mechanisms, however with her learning disability— *(sudden cut-off of music)*

LANNI: My WHAT?

BETH: It's nothing new, Lanni. You've probably had this all your life. Children who have learning disorders have at least average abilities for thinking and learning, and you've certainly demonstrated that. You're a bright girl. *(high plucking note of a violin or perhaps quick angelic chord of a harp)*

LANNI: Oh, okay.

BETH: Learning disabilities simply affect the *(repeat earlier lulling classical music)* acquisition, organization, retention…

LANNI: Just more of Beige Beth's gobbledygook. I'm thinking it's all okay when "WHAM!" Suddenly I'm ducking a puck shot at 100 miles an hour — sorry, that'd be…well, you figure out how fast in kilometres per hour.

BETH: She'd benefit from a special class. Resource room.

LANNI: Nah, unuuh. No. Special Class. Dude, it's not an option. Cool kids don't do stuff like that. Hockey players don't do stuff like that or get high grades. Okay, okay. So I had a few stereotypes there. Whaddaya expect, I was a kid.

Beige Beth — who had changed it up into a beige suit with a brown blouse today, by the way — started talking about how it would help my learning. I hear Mum say, "Well, if you're sure this will help and won't just label her…"

BETH: These children have been taught that we all learn in different ways. There's no stigma involved. It will help her self-esteem.

LANNI: Self-esteem? Didn't have much left after I'd been labelled a "dummy." *(pretends to punch someone, then help pick them up and dust them off)* The first time a guy called me a dummy, I punched him. Then I apologized because I was too dumb to know any better. He didn't dare tell because he'd be in trouble for name-calling. After that no one called me names again. At least to my face. Yeah. I could protect myself. But I'd have preferred invisibility. Since they had the power play, I fell back on the things I'd learned on the ice. Distraction. Individual style of play. It had always worked for me. Like with this one opponent. I had to work really hard to stay with her. She had great speed and an awesome shot, but she used to get really thrown when I sang "Happy Birthday" to her. *(sings)* "Happy birthday to you…happy birthday, dear #12, happy birthday to you." She'd totally lose her focus and look at me.

PLAYER: It isn't my birthday.

LANNI: And…whoops. She missed the pass. Oh, well. Better luck next time, hotshot.

           So, Coach, my plan was to work really hard where no one could see me, so I got to school early and worked in the desk outside the principal's office. Ms. Norsdale gave me a few pointers. The Resource Room teacher said my work had improved and I could just drop in once a week. Yes! Then Ms. Norsdale gave me some sports questions — a puck going 100 mph is doing 160 kph just in case you're wondering. Finally, in grade 8, she gave me one big assignment. But, dude, it was the most amazing assignment. I was covering a Team Canada vs. Team USA game, and I had to make the whole thing up. It was great.

Ms. N: What period are we in, Lanni?

LANNI: *(using ANNOUNCER's voice)* End of the second period, ladies and gentlemen. It's anyone's game.

Ms. N: The score?

LANNI: *(using ANNOUNCER's voice)* Team Canada and Team USA have battled to a one-one tie.

Ms. N: Show me where these players are from on the map. Good job.

LANNI: Then it got more complicated.

Ms. N: What's the composition of the different hockey sticks? Mmhmm. Okay. Now let's do some stats…

LANNI: I realized I knew a lot of…stuff! I guess Ms. Norsdale thought so, too, because she gave me an A+ that counted on my final report card. Maybe I could even be a sportscaster someday. *(using ANNOUNCER's voice)* Ladies and gentlemen, the player almost turned a cartwheel. Wait. *(she turns a cartwheel)* I did turn a cartwheel.

           High school. Freshman year. No remedial classes. *(low note.)* No hated subjects like spelling and handwriting, *(higher note)* no girl/boy segregation and no long lists of rules, *(highest note)* just a simple little handbook. *(full chord)* Yes. The teachers treated us more like adults, like our principal, Mr. Peters. He seemed to know all the older students and what they were involved in. He was busy making contacts with the new grade nines, and since I was often *(sashays, does the popular student routine)* in the centre of the group, he made it a point to know my name and banter.

MR. P: All right, students, look lively. The bell is about to ring. You don't want to be known as Late Lanni.

LANNI: Hey, Mr. Peters. Step into our classroom for a few minutes to liven it up, and I wouldn't want to be late.

MR. P: You don't want me in your classroom, Lanni. You might actually have to do some work.

LANNI: Oh, Mr. Peters. I'm a regular workaholic. And I gave him a little salute. He laughed and saluted right back.

Then, I tried out for the high school volleyball team, which is a great way to stay sharp before hockey starts. I made the team — freshman year, can you imagine? Mr. Peters really liked to talk about that, and the other kids all gathered around and thought it was cool. I was popular and accepted and…this cute guy named Regan had started to notice me.

The first set of report cards came out. My grades were mostly Cs, with a couple of Bs. Math and Science were a D… I passed! *(does the Wayne Gretzky pump, or variation)* Except at the bottom of the report card was a little zinger, handwritten by the principal. "You've got to learn to apply yourself. Try harder." Hey, on the one hand, he's noticed me. Checking to see how I'm doing. That's cool. Right? But…

But there's more. Today, I'm in the cafeteria. It's nearly the end of the volleyball season and a whole bunch of us are talking about the big tournament on the weekend. I notice Regan move to our table, and I'm hoping he'll find a way to sit next to me. And then Mr. Peters comes in.

MR. P: Good to see our top athletes filling up on nutritious cafeteria food before the big tournament. Fries are always a great athletic choice. Hey, young lady.

LANNI: And he actually points.

MR. P: Work up to your potential or you might have played your last game this year.

LANNI: In front of everyone, even Regan. Especially Regan. It gets worse. He pulls out the Student Handbook, flips a couple of pages and reads.

MR. P: This goes for all of you. "Athletes are expected to maintain a 60% average or better, with no uncleared lates or absences."

LANNI: He peers right at me over the top of the book.

MR. P: We expect our top athletes to pay attention to academics, too. Lanni, your marks just got you benched for the tournament this weekend.

LANNI: I feel like there's a giant crack in the ice and I've just landed on my face. I wish the crack would open wider and I could disappear. A bunch of the kids that have classes with me look at me kind of funny. First thought? Geez, she seems to work harder and longer than anybody. Second thought — does she ever answer questions in class? Third thought — Hey, she does her homework. Fourth thought? Yeah, this time there's time for a fourth thought. And it's wonky. Something is wonky here. Good thing I'd been yelled at by a coach or two, or I might've cried. But I don't cry. Instead, I say, "Mr. Peters, don't get all worked up now. It'd be bad luck on your birthday." And a bunch of kids start talking about how maybe they should give him the royal bumps for his birthday, and Mr. Peters is sputtering.

MR. P: It's not my birthday, it's—

LANNI: (sings) Happy birthday to you…happy birthday, Mr. Peters… And when everybody joins in singing and cracking jokes, I get the heck out of there. It's so unfair, Coach. I want to play so much. (angrily sings) Happy Birthday to you. Happy Birthday, Mr. Peters. Happy Birthday to you. What's next, hockey? Why does my mark in science or math mean I have to have something I love taken away from me? What about the kid that's a math whiz but can't even skate? Does he ever get his calculator taken away until he does a skating drill properly? I'm so angry. Try harder. Will my "trying harder" ever be good enough? I might as well drop out. I don't belong here. I leave the school and take off to the rink. As I put on my skates, I notice the callouses on the little fingers of my hand from tightening my skate laces. Put pressure on something and it toughens up. A callous is not such a bad thing to have as you go through life, maybe.

I shoot puck after puck after puck. *(she shoots to coincide with memory, as angry background music plays, such as intro to "Loco" by Coal Chamber, and we hear pucks bouncing off the boards)* At first I remember Mr. Raznik and his mean comments, and Ms. W. ripping up my paper and Beige Beth testing and testing me, and having the kids call me dummy when I went to the Resource Room. I remember how hard I worked on my own to pass my high school classes. I think about being humiliated in front of everyone in the cafeteria. I wonder if Regan will still look at me like I'm something special. I keep on shooting, until I'm in the zone, you know? *(music changes to soft music, or a Zen/rock rhythmic sound)* My movements become smooth and fluid. And then I think about learning to read, my coaches and teammates, my family support and my superior scores on some of the tests, doing great on Ms. Norsdale's assignments and passing high school classes. I play sports well and I can talk to the guys. Not everybody can do that stuff. Beige Beth is right. I am bright. I've made it this far, right? But it…this learning disability… isn't going away. Big deal. I don't make it to the other end of the ice on my own in a hockey game. Yeah, Coach. I've got a game plan. My mind is made up. I'm going back to that school, and I'm going to play in that volleyball tournament, somehow.

When I came out here to the rink I was ripped up inside. So where's the sticky tape? What holds me together the way that tape held my ripped up assignment together, or the way hockey tape holds my stick together and holds my socks up?

For some of you, it might be ballet, a perfect stone to skip across the water, a little dog licking your face, or the aroma of freshly baked cookies.

But my sticky tape? It's what happens inside me when there's a pair of sharp skates, a stick with perfect flex and weight, a round black puck and a sheet of freshly cleaned ice. I skate out here listening to the sss sss sing of my blades biting the ice as I lengthen my stride. I feel the whoosh of the finely balanced stick in my hands, the slight taaang as the stick meets the puck and responds to my movement. Then, I feel the tension in my muscles as I let that puck go, and the thrill of the smack as it lands in the back of the net. Oooh, yeah.

> *She exits, as we hear* ANNOUNCER *say "She shoots, she scores!"*

The End

Production History

First produced at the 2006 University of Regina Student Infringement under the name *Skool Days Not So Kool Days*

Director	David McBride
Stage Manager	Allene Chernick
Lanni	Megan Leach

The second production, now called *Learning the Game* (Spring, 2008) by Ice Time Theatre Collective (Regina, SK) toured throughout Saskatchewan as part of the Organization of Saskatchewan Arts Councils (OSAC) Youth Tour. Then Ice Time Theatre Collective took it on a Western Canadian Fringe Tour (Summer, 2008) to Winnipeg, Regina, Saskatoon, Edmonton and Vancouver.

Director	John D. Huston
Stage Manager	Simon Moccasin
Lanni	Megan Leach

Acknowledgements

I am grateful to the Saskatchewan Playwrights Centre and its dramaturges Ben Henderson and Heather Inglis for their support in the development of this play. An early draft called *Skool Days Not So Kool Days* was first staged at the University of Regina's Student Infringement with dramaturgy by Janet Amos, performed by Megan Leach, directed by David McBride and stage managed by Allene Chernick. Thanks to workshop actors Megan Leach and Cheryl Jack and to Don List (Birdsong Communications Ltd.) for their assistance and belief in the developmental process. Marianne Woods and the Organization of Saskatchewan Arts Councils gave us the opportunity to tour this play across Saskatchewan (Spring 2008) with performer Megan Leach, director John D. Huston and stage manager Simon Moccasin. Megan's enthusiasm for the piece brought the play to the Fringe in Western Canada (Summer 2008.) Thanks, too, to family, friends, fellow writers and audience members who offered advice, support and insights. With assistance from the Canada Arts Council.

About the Playwright

Janice Salkeld primarily writes plays (*StreetZone*, Sarasvati Theatre 2005, *I Need a Piece*, North Battleford Players, 2004) but has had some poetry and short stories published in various anthologies such as *Grain* magazine. Before becoming a writer Janice enjoyed working as a junior high/high school teacher and as a program coordinator/consultant for Early Childhood Intervention Programs. She lived many years in NWT and YT before returning to her home province of Saskatchewan, where she now resides in Saskatoon.

Interview

Lanni arrived on my writing pages one day, and I thought I might write a poem or short story about her, but she was so dynamic I soon realized I wanted to put her on stage. I wanted to show things from her point of view, not as helpless and hopeless, but rather as resilient; not always right, but solving problems as best she can, frustrated but still confident that she is good at many things. Part of my objective was to show others how it *feels* to have a learning disability, not to simply read a definition. It felt like Lanni should be a female character, because there are often different expectations for girls than there are for boys. Finally, having been strongly influenced by storytelling traditions, and wanting to keep this story personal and intimately Lanni's, I chose to write it as a monologue.

Working on the play generated discussion on a lot of issues, and picking and choosing was difficult. I had one eye on the length, wanting it to be suitable for a range of ages and for tight school schedules, and wanting to allow time for discussion after the show if possible.

Because of all the things that Lanni was struggling with, I chose to reveal them in layers. The timeline with the standard flashback technique is straightforward. Lanni comes onstage obviously upset with a problem, reviews how she got there, and decides on a course of action. But I wanted a pattern of circular events within the linear structure, and to create the feeling that Lanni's story goes on.

The use of the language and terminology of learning disabilities is often a sensitive issue. I chose to use what is currently in use in my area. (Example: resource room.) Obviously there will be regional differences in terms and language, but I've done my best with the information available to me at this time.

Part of what I love about theatre is the involvement and cooperation of so many people. In addition to the actor, director and stage manager, this play has made quite a journey through and with the community. It started with fellow writers at Sage Hill, and my writing group. After reading my first draft, they asked how long I had spent researching it. I told them about 15 years...being a hockey mom was pretty intense research. Working with dramaturges, including readings and workshops, was woven throughout the play's development and was invaluable.

The first performance, then called *Skool Days Not So Kool Days,* was done in front of a primarily university crowd. The dress rehearsal for the Youth Tour was performed in a church with a largely senior audience. *Learning the Game's* tours went from small isolated villages to large cities, from schools to the Fringe, and even included a performance at a hockey wind-up! As I said, that's quite a path through the community. Throughout this time, the actor, Megan Leach, kept giving me feedback from her point of view and from the audience. I was also able to see some shows myself, and I kept working on the script. I never made sweeping changes — the premise of the play stayed the same — but characters and concepts were added and dropped, tightening the whole flow of the piece.

For me, personally, it was exciting to attend a performance at Twin Lakes School in Buffalo Narrows, Saskatchewan, where I used to teach, and feel I was giving something back to a community that had given me so much.

There were a couple of unexpectedly tough moments, too. In one school a teenage boy got up and walked out. After the show, a teacher came over and told me it had hit rather too close to home. In other instances some students have been quite emotional after the show. I was also struck by the number of kids who want to talk and open the conversation with "my cousin, my friend, my sister has a learning disability and…" At the Fringe, with more family and adult audiences, there were a lot of comments about this play being a starting point to generate discussion…and sometimes relief that some of the issues that learning disabled kids and their families deal with were being addressed.

Instead of writing with a particular actor in mind, I wrote this play with a particular audience in mind. I tried to write the show that I'd like to take my own kids to. They were also my "go-to" people for correct hockey terminology, assistance with the computer, and honest feedback…my own elite coaches! Thanks, guys.

To Be Frank

by Brian Drader

Characters

FRANK — assistant editor, school newspaper
EMMA — editor, school newspaper
DAD — Frank's father
MS. WINTHROW — school principal
MR. ENDLE — the chemistry teacher

Playwright's Notes

To Be Frank is written for four or five actors. The parts of Mr. Endle and Frank's dad could be played by the same actor.

There are school newspaper and web site messages throughout the play. The newspaper messages are identified as BULLETIN BOARD, the web site messages as MESSAGE BOARD. They could be treated as an audio element, and possibly amplified or distorted to establish and enhance them as separate from real time. They might also be treated as a visual element, possibly using projection, or an oversized (i.e. simulated) computer screen. "******" in the later MESSAGE BOARD postings is intentional censorship, and could be handled with either a "bleep" if it were an audio component, or as is if it were a visual component.

The playing area is open to interpretation.

School buzzer sounds.

FRANK, in a hurry, wrestling with an unruly mound of folders and proofs and papers and computer disks.

He stops, takes in the audience.

FRANK: Okay, like, I've been thinking about…
…ah, forget it.

He continues on his way. He stops.

Okay. Look. It's not like it's any big deal, it's just I don't want you getting the wrong idea about why I might be thinking about the thing I'm thinking about. All the porn. On the Net. Have you ever looked at all that stuff? Well, like, obviously not all of it, your eyeballs would burn out of your head if you looked at all of it there's so frickin' much, but you know what I mean, have you ever checked it out? It's right there, you don't have to pay for it. I mean I guess there's REAL porn if you pay for it, but the ads are enough, you know? They show everything, and all sorts of crap that doesn't even have anything to do with sex, it's just freaky. And it's right there. Click click bam. You don't even have to look for it, I mean they send you links in your hotmail without you even asking. As soon as I got on the Net I checked it out, 'cause it's…well, 'cause it's there, right? So of course I'm going to take a look and of course my dad, this is my stepdad, not my blood dad, of course he walks into my room just as I'm checkin' out this site, and I try to click out real quick, right? But it's wired to all these other sites, so every time I close one, three more pop up, and I don't know where they're all coming from, it's like a nightmare, I can't click 'em down fast enough, and my dad's just standing there watching me and I thought I was going to die. He shut me down. Took me off the Net for a month. And he gave me the big lecture on the evils of pornography and how those people doing all that stuff to each other are strangers and they're getting paid to do it, most of the time anyway, sometimes they're not even paid, they're forced to do it, I mean there's some pretty scary stuff out there, you know? But anyway he's telling me how sex is all healthy between two people who love

each other but those people don't even know each other
and blah blah blah blah blah like I don't already know all
that, I'd seen porn before. Yeah, it's all hangin' out and you
can see everything so big whoopee deal. It's nothing new.
And the kind of stuff you see on the Net most of it's just
a big boring perv freak show anyway, but of course my
dad thinks I'm in there to get my rocks off. What else is
he going to think, right? So I gotta get the big love and
sex talk, which is just weird, it's just weird talking to your
parents about that kinda stuff. It just is. Even when they're
cool, and he's cool, it's still weird, 'cause as soon as they
start talking about it you can't pretend anymore that they
don't do it, and I don't want to think about my parents
doin' it. It's just too weird.

I don't mind yakkin' with my dad about other stuff. It's
crazy what's going on out there, you roam around the
Net, and there's so much happening, not just the porn,
I'm talkin' about all the things going on in the world, the
wars, and the inventions, and all the stuff that's for sale, it's
like the whole world's for sale, and all the crazy weather,
and the ozone is depleting at some unreal rate and we're
all going to fry if we don't drown from the floods first,
and we're eating genetically altered foods and using pigs
to grow replacement parts for ourselves, and pretty soon
we're going to be growing ourselves to use as replacement
parts for ourselves, and we're turning the whole planet
into some giant garbage dump, and there are all these
huge diseases like AIDS and E-coli bacteria and killer bees
and it all doesn't matter anyway 'cause we're going to blow
ourselves up with some nuclear disaster before the killer
bees get us. Sometimes I look at all that stuff and I don't
want to grow up, ya know? I just want to goof around and
hang with my friends, and go to parties and watch TV in
my gontch and just not think about it. But it's impossible.
It's comin' at you from everywhere, and we're expected to
deal with all this adult crap in an adult way, but we're still
treated like kids. I mean, really. Think about it. It's like we
just outgrew the chemistry set and now we're supposed to
build a bomb. It's no wonder so many of us blow ourselves
up. So I don't mind yakkin' with my dad. He's decent. He

gets it. Except he's always telling me I think too much. Just stay in the moment, you know? The here. The now. Ooohmmmm. My mom and my dad were both hippies when they were younger. I mean, they're still hippies, but they got short hair now. They had to get jobs, I guess. Anyway, they both got that livin' day to day "in the now" thing down pretty good. This is my stepdad I'm talkin' about. My blood dad, he doesn't think that way at all. I think that's why he's rich.

Oh yeah. I'm Frank. Well, my real name is François, but everyone calls me Frank. François was my blood dad's name. I go visit him in Montreal once a year, but that's about it, so it's not weird having the same name, except every once in a while Mom'll talk about when he used to live with us, and I can see why he'd get on her nerves, he is pretty uptight, but every once in a while Mom will say that uptight, stick-up-the-arse François and a few other choice little words that I'd get in deep shit for saying here. Oh. Sorry. I shouldn't say shit either. But anyway, Mom would be trashing him and I'm like, uh, excuse me, Mom? I'm right here? It's my name too? And she'd feel all bad and then I'd feel bad, but we'd laugh it off. She's pretty cool.

She told me I could change it if I wanted to. Four years ago. It was on all the lists at school, the attendance and stuff, and when a teacher would call it out, "François McBarrister," like what is that, it's like a United Nations car wreck, and I hated it. It just made me feel stupid 'cause everybody would giggle and snicker and I didn't get the joke, I guess, so four years ago for my thirteenth birthday my mom told me I could change it. I could pick any name I wanted. So I called myself Raw Lee Ice T. I actually spent a whole day telling people to call me that, but obviously it didn't last too long, I got beat up at recess. So I'm trying to think of another name, what I want to call myself, and I can't think of myself with any other name but Frank, it's what I am, and I start to think that maybe it's okay that I've got this other name, François, this secret name that's another part of me. The part that doesn't live out loud, you know? The part you keep to yourself.

And it sounds a lot cooler when you hear it walkin' down a street in Montreal. François. It works there. So I told Mom I'd keep it. We took it off all the school stuff, but I kept it on my birth certificate. She gave me the computer for my birthday instead. She's pretty cool.

Shit. What am I doin'? I'm late. Gotta go.

> *Frank tears off, papers and folders and proofs and disks barely in hand.*

Bulletin Board

Attention all students—
There will be a general assembly on Monday the 11th, following morning attendance.

An open invitation.
Anyone interested in signing up for the horticulturist's society, our first meeting will be in Room #138 at 4:00 on Tuesday the 12th. Feel free to bring your favourite plant! Contact Lisa Rebo for more details.

> *School buzzer sounds.*

> *Emma breezes by. Frank pursues, his administrative hell still in tow. He is now dropping as much as he manages to hold onto.*

FRANK: Emma. Wait up.

EMMA: I'm late for student council.

FRANK: So what? You're the president. They've gotta wait for you.

EMMA: I'm not going to make them wait just because I can. Aren't you supposed to be at the printers'?

FRANK: There's some stuff I forgot to go over with you at lunch.

EMMA: What stuff?

FRANK: Just slow down, okay? It'll only take a minute.

EMMA: I don't have a minute. You're the assistant editor. You can make decisions.

FRANK: Yeah, like you say that, and then every time I do make a decision you change it, or tell me it's wrong.

EMMA: That's not true.

FRANK: Yes it is.

EMMA: Not.

FRANK: I spent a whole day on the front page, you took one look at it, and canned it.

EMMA: It wasn't a front page. It was an eight-and-a-half by eleven full-colour glossy of two polished, heaving, barely contained and unnaturally large breasts.

FRANK: I thought we could make it the swimsuit issue.

EMMA: It's a school newspaper. We don't have a swimsuit issue.

FRANK: Well. There it is. Why don't we have a swimsuit issue? Throw a hottie on the cover. Get the guys interested.

          Silence.

          What?

EMMA: It never occurred to you that putting a surgically enhanced, airbrushed, bikini-clad sex puff on the cover of our school newspaper might possibly offend a few people?

FRANK: C'mon, Em. Loosen up. I was just havin' some fun.

EMMA: Why didn't you use a picture of a half-naked guy?

FRANK: Why would I do that?

EMMA: My point exactly.

          EMMA begins to leave.

FRANK: What point? You didn't make a point. Wait! There's still stuff I need to ask you about.

EMMA: I'm late.

          FRANK shuffles through a hurricane of paper, trying to hold onto everything as he searches the various files.

FRANK: It's okay. I'll be quick. I got it right here…nope…nope…is that?…nope.

          Ms. WINTHROW, the school principal, is heard over the intercom.

Ms. W:　　Emma Hogan to the student council room, please. Emma to the student council room.

EMMA:　　Oh great. Look, you're going to have to take care of it yourself, okay?

FRANK:　　Wait! Just one thing…here. We got a letter in yesterday, I forgot to show it to you. Take a look…

He manages to pass her a piece of paper. She begins to read it.

EMMA:　　This is an English assignment.

FRANK:　　Hmm?

EMMA shows it to him.

Oh crap. I was supposed to hand that in yesterday. Better put that in the priority file. Could you…just…it's just under my right arm here…

She stuffs the paper in wherever.

Yeah, that's… Thanks. Okay. The letter. It's right…oh, here, here. This is it. Take a look at this.

He manages to hand her another piece of paper. She begins to read.

EMMA:　　What is this?

FRANK:　　It's a letter to the editor, taking a strip off Mr. Endle, the Chem teacher.

EMMA:　　Incompetent…boring…mean-spirited… Who wrote this?

FRANK:　　It wasn't signed.

EMMA:　　So what do you want me to do with it?

FRANK:　　Should we run it?

EMMA:　　Of course not.

FRANK:　　Oh. I kinda already put it in. I thought it might be controversial, you know?

EMMA: That's a reason to print it? C'mon, Frank. You print it because it's a legitimate opinion expressed by one of the students, and this is a student newspaper. Unfortunately, this student doesn't have the guts to sign it, so we don't print it. That's the policy.

FRANK: Yeah, but the issue is really boring. We need some juice, you know? Something to stir it up a bit. And I figured… well, it's Endle. It's true. He's a lousy teacher.

EMMA: We can't start printing unsigned letters to the editor. For all anybody knows, we could just be making them up.

FRANK: Yeah, I guess…

EMMA: You've still got time to pull the letter and clean it all up, but you better get a move on. The printers need everything by 4:30 if we want it out on Monday. Okay?

FRANK: Yeah. Okay.

EMMA: Later.

          EMMA leaves. FRANK gathers up the papers and folders and computer disks he's dropped. He addresses the audience. Through the following, his gathering evolves into him cleaning up at home, talking to himself.

FRANK: I can't believe how stupid she makes me feel sometimes. It's because she's always thought it through, you know? It doesn't matter what it is, she's always got the right answer. When does she have time to think about all this stuff?

          FRANK's DAD is passing, stops, watches his son.

          It's not like I don't try. I think about stuff, but it's like I got the attention span of a dog. Oh. Look at that. Bored. Oh. Look at this. Bored. Oh. Let's look at that again. Bored. Man. I gotta get a datebook, or a watch or something. Something to keep me on track, you know? That's the problem. I never write things down, and then I get all bunged down in all the details, because I'm trying to keep it all in my head, and then some dumb thing that has nothing to do with anything comes boomin' in from left field and the whole thing disintegrates, and I can't even remember what I was supposed to be doing. I'm left with a head full of junk and no place to put it.

DAD: You okay?

FRANK: Aaaah! Dad! You scared the crap out of me.

DAD: You losin' it?

FRANK: I'm just talking to myself. Something wrong with that?

DAD: No, I guess not. How's it coming?

FRANK: How clean does it gotta be?

DAD: Have to be.

FRANK: Have to be what?

DAD: How clean does it have to be.

FRANK: That's what I'm asking.

DAD: It's have to be, not gotta be.

FRANK: Dad!

DAD: What!

FRANK: It's the weekend. I can't be expected to learn 24/7. Gimme a break, why don't ya.

DAD: What's your problem?

FRANK: Nothin'.

DAD: Then why are you being so snippy?

FRANK: I'm just sick and tired of being stupid all the time.

DAD: You're not stupid.

FRANK: I can't keep two thoughts in my head without them getting mixed up. It's like I'm a friggin' crack baby hooked on espresso or something, except of course I wouldn't know what that was like but that's what I think it would be like, that's what I feel like, except I shouldn't be makin' fun of crack babies, I know that, I'm not makin' fun of them, I don't mean / anything by it, I'm just trying to explain what's goin' on in my head, you know?

DAD: / Just…Frank…Frank… Relax!

Man. You get yourself so keyed up about everything, like you have to think about it all at once. You don't. One thing at a time. Right here. That's all there is. Just stay in the room. Relax.

FRANK: Yeah, but it doesn't always work like that. It can't always be about "the moment." Sometimes you have to look ahead and see what's coming, or or maybe look back so you can see how something ended up the way it did or if you don't it just sits there anyway and mumbles like white noise in your brain and you can't focus on anything and you're all distracted because you think maybe you don't care enough or you're too lazy or too afraid or not smart enough or strong enough to deal with it so you have to go back to it anyway whatever it was so how am I supposed to stay "in the moment" with all that going on in my head? Huh? It's no wonder I screw up all the time.

DAD: Your mom says you have highly receptive neurons. Maybe she's right. Maybe you've got some kind of mutant alien super brain.

FRANK: Yeah, well, if that's the case it's not exactly showing up on my report card.

DAD: I know. I've seen your report card.

Look, Frank, I don't know what makes you the way you are. But I do know you're a smart kid. Maybe it doesn't show up in your school work, but it's there. I see it. You just think differently than a lot of people. Or some. Some people. I mean, it's not like there's something wrong with you. It's not that you think differently in a bad way, you think differently in a good way. You're…well, different, yes, but in a good way. You're an individual. Which is not to say that you're alone. You're unique, we're all unique, but that doesn't mean alone. There are lots of people who think like you do. We just…don't know any of them.

This isn't really helping, is it?

FRANK: No. Good try, though. Hey, how about you help me clean up? That would make me feel better.

              DAD stares at him a moment...

              ...and exits.

Dad?

              FRANK shrugs it off and goes back to gathering his stuff, corralling the rest with his feet, herding it off.

BULLETIN BOARD

To Amanda Dillan from Rachel Cuddy — I didn't appreciate you telling W. that I had a thing for N. It's not true, and anyway, even if it was, it's nothing N. or W. needed to know about. We are officially not friends anymore, so don't like even bother.

BULLETIN BOARD

For Sale. One used nose ring. Make me an offer. Sam in Rm. 206.

BULLETIN BOARD

Hello out there, plant lovers! Where are you? It seems none of you were able to attend the horticulturist society's last meeting. Fortunately my schedule is fairly free, so we can try another day. How about Tuesday the 19th, 4:00, Room #138 (that's the biology lab, in case anyone got lost last time). "Liatrame" (*lee a tra me*) know if you can't make it! "Salicaceae" (*sal a see ya*) there!
Lisa Rebo.
P.S. If you're not sure what Liatrame and Salicaceae mean, come to the meeting and find out!

              School buzzer sounds.

              We hear EMMA, off stage.

EMMA: Frank!

              FRANK comes tearing on, obviously trying to avoid EMMA. She is in hot pursuit.

Frank...

FRANK: Em! Hi! Look. Sorry. Gotta run. I'm...you know...late, for...stuff. Gotta go.

EMMA: How did the letter that I specifically told you to pull end up in the paper?

FRANK: How was your weekend?

EMMA: Do you know how much trouble we're in? The whole school is talking about it. I saw Mr. Endle in the hall this morning. He told me straight out he's lodging a complaint with Winthrow. Why didn't you pull it?

FRANK: I was going to. But I was late getting to the printer, and there was still stuff I had to make decisions on 'cause you took off to the student council meeting and by the time I got through all / that stuff...

EMMA: / All what stuff? What else was there?

FRANK: I had to...you know...okay, so there wasn't really that much, but I was late and I ran into a couple of friends on the way and got to yakkin' and by the time I got to the printer they were closing and I had to talk them into taking the stuff and I forgot to pull the letter.

EMMA: I should have known better.

FRANK: What does that mean?

EMMA: It means if I wanted it done right, I should have just done it myself.

FRANK: You don't have to get nasty. I just forgot.

We hear Ms. WINTHROW over the intercom.

Ms. W: Emma Hogan to the office, please. Emma Hogan to the office.

EMMA: Great. Here we go.

FRANK: I'll come with you. I'll tell her it was my fault.

EMMA: We'll print an apology to Mr. Endle in the next issue. That should make everybody happy.

FRANK: Yeah.

EMMA: I'm not trying to be nasty, Frank. But it was a pretty big mistake, you know? You're a smart guy. There's no reason you shouldn't be more on top of things. You just have to pay attention.

FRANK: I'm not you.

EMMA: Excuse me?

FRANK: It's not as important to me, okay? To be honest, I don't really give a shit about the stupid paper. It's more trouble than it's worth.

EMMA: So why are you doing this?

FRANK: Because I wanted to spend more time with you. I thought it'd be fun.

            Silence.

EMMA: Look. I understand that maybe this stuff isn't all that important to you, but it is important to me.

            I know people talk about me. Behind my back. They call me brainiac and little miss perfect, and a lot worse. I'm starting to figure out that's the way it goes. It's like a guarantee. I'm good at organizing people and getting things done, and some people like me for that, but a lot of people don't. They think it's some kind of power trip, or that I must be all full of myself, or just because I'm a girl and I'm not afraid to take charge I must be a bitch.

FRANK: Emma…

EMMA: That's what they call me. I'm not deaf. Okay. Fine. I can't make everybody like me. I can deal with that. But then all that's left is to do a good job, right? For the people who do appreciate it. And for myself, so that at the end of the day I can say I'm worth something.

            All I'm asking is if you're going to help, pay attention, and if you're going to slough off, I'd rather you just tell me now, and I'll do it myself, okay?

FRANK: I'm sorry.

EMMA: It's okay. Nobody died. And the rest of the issue looks great. C'mon. Let's get this over with.

EMMA exits.

FRANK begins to follow, stops, addresses the audience.

FRANK: She totally wants me.

He continues on his way, stops again.

It's weird, you know? The way things change sometimes. Emma and I have been hangin' out since grade seven. We lived beside each other, so we just ended up best friends. It just happened. And five years go by, and I'm lookin' at her now, and...well, things just change, you know? Hey, did you hear what she said about the rest of the issue? Pretty fly for a dumb guy, eh? You know, I figure if I just get a watch, I got this whole game licked. Maybe I don't even need one. I'm getting pretty good at guessing what time it is. I don't need a clock to wake up in the morning any more.

As soon as the sun comes up, bam, I'm there, even if the room's pitch black, it's automatic, like I'm connected to it or something. I can stay up all night, crash, get an hour's sleep, the sun comes up, bam, I'm awake, and...um...what was...oh crap.

FRANK tears off after EMMA.

Lights shift to Ms. WINTHROW, MR. ENDLE, and EMMA, in Ms. WINTHROW's office.

Ms. W: Thanks for coming to see us, Emma. Please, come in. Have a seat.

EMMA takes a seat as FRANK comes running into the office, out of breath.

FRANK: Sorry, Ms. Winthrow.

Ms. W: Excuse me?

FRANK: Sorry I'm late. Just carry on. I'm okay.

Ms. W: And you are...

FRANK: Frank.

     Silence.

     McBarrister.

Ms. W: Can I help you with something?

EMMA: He's my assistant editor.

Ms. W: There's no need for you both to be here.

EMMA: I asked him to come along.

Ms. W: Suit yourself. You both know Mr. Endle, I trust.

MR. E: Emma. Frank.

EMMA: Mr. Endle.

FRANK: Sorry about the letter there, Mr. E.

MR. E: Yes, well, that's why we're here, isn't it?

Ms. W: I was surprised you printed it, Emma.

FRANK: No, you / see…

Ms. W: / You usually show such good judgement.

FRANK: No, see, it wasn't like that. What happened / was…

Ms. W: / Fred, if you don't / mind…

FRANK: / Frank.

Ms. W: Pardon?

FRANK: My name's Frank.

Ms. W: Yes, well, Frank, if you insist on interrupting I'll have to ask you to leave.

FRANK: But I just wanted you to / understand…

Ms. W: / You'll have your turn.

EMMA: It's okay, Frank.

Ms. W: As I was saying, I'm surprised at you, Emma. The content of the letter was completely unfounded, and on top of that it was anonymous. We don't publish unsigned letters.

EMMA: You mean the newspaper.

Ms. W: Pardon?

EMMA: You said "we" don't publish unsigned letters. I assume you
          meant the newspaper.

Ms. W: I'm not quite sure that I understand the distinction you're
          making here, Ms. Hogan.

EMMA: The newspaper belongs to the students, it doesn't belong
          to you.

          Silence.

Ms. W: I don't think we need to get into ownership issues here.
          The fact remains that the letter was unsigned, and our
          editorial policy clearly / states that…

EMMA: / Ms. Winthrow, I'm not disagreeing with you. I'm very
          aware of what our editorial policy is, and I'm certainly
          willing to honour it. But I want to make sure we're clear
          that the newspaper answers to the students, not the
          teachers. It's their paper, not yours.

Ms. W: Perhaps I'm not making myself clear. The letter was
          inappropriate, you were wrong in printing it, and you're
          going to have to print an apology.

FRANK: Okay, well, see, this shouldn't be a problem, 'cause Emma
          and I were already talking about / this, and we…

EMMA: / What do you mean "have to"? What if we can find the
          student who wrote the letter?

Ms. W: Then he or she can write the apology.

EMMA: It's a letter to the editor. It's one student's opinion,
          expressed in the proper forum. If we can find who wrote
          it, and they're willing to take responsibility for it, then why
          couldn't we run it?

Ms. W: I will not tolerate the newspaper criticising the teachers.
          It's hostile and damaging and it benefits no one. And
          need I remind you, Emma, that the majority of the
          newspaper's budget comes from the school, not the
          student body.

EMMA: What if the teacher deserves it?

FRANK: Look, Ms. Winthrow, this really isn't a problem. / You see...

EMMA: / No. It's a legitimate question. What if the teacher deserves it?

MR. E: You think I deserved to be called those names? That I'm a boring teacher? Incompetent?

EMMA: I've taken your class. The letter went too far, but it wasn't unfounded.

FRANK: Emma! What are / you doing?

MR. E: / You best watch yourself, young lady.

EMMA: Tell me, Mr. Endle, when's the last time you helped a student outside of class?

MR. E: That's none of your business.

EMMA: Okay, fine. How about the last time you ventured outside of the teacher's manual. Have you ever done your own class plan?

MR. E: This is hardly the time or the place to be discussing my performance as a teacher.

EMMA: I suppose you're right. After all, this is a school, and we are on school hours. It's hardly the time or the place.

MS. W: That is enough! You apologize to Mr. Endle this instant.

EMMA: No! You're being completely unfair. Maybe that letter wasn't signed, but it was the truth. If the students can't print the truth in their own newspaper, then what's the point?

MR. E: Did you write that letter?

EMMA: And what if I did?

FRANK: Whoa. Okay. This is getting weird. Look, Ms. Winthrow, Mr. E, see, what happened / was...

MS. W: / Did you?

FRANK: No, see, Emma didn't have anything to do with this whole / thing...

Ms. W: / Did you write that letter?

Silence.

I can't possibly express how disappointed I am in you. I want the remaining copies of the newspaper pulled from the school, and a front page apology, written by you, in the next issue. Understood?

EMMA: Or what?

Ms. W: Or I close down the newspaper.

EMMA: You can't do that!

Ms. W: I most certainly can, and I will.

I'm going to give you a day to think about this, Ms. Hogan. But my decision is final. I'd suggest you come around, or you will lose the paper.

EMMA gets up and leaves the office. FRANK follows, babbling on the way out.

FRANK: This didn't go at all like...see, we were, well, it was my fault to begin with and...Emma! Wait up!...and and we were gonna...well, I don't know what just happened, but I'll talk to her, I'm sure it'll be fine. Thanks for your time. Really. Appreciate it. Have a great day. Both of you. Just have a...great day, and I'll talk to Emma, and we'll get this all worked out, 'kay?

Silence.

Emma!

FRANK tears out of the office. Lights fade on Ms. WINTHROW and MR. ENDLE.

FRANK catches up to EMMA in the hallway.

FRANK: What was that?

EMMA: Did you hear her?

FRANK: I don't know what I heard. What happened? I thought we were okay with the apology. I thought that was the plan. Did I miss a memo or something?

EMMA: She can't do that. She can't just shut down the paper because she doesn't agree with the content.

FRANK: Uh, yes she can. And by the sounds of it, she will. I don't see what the big problem is. She's asking you to do what you already planned to do.

EMMA: She's not asking me to do anything. She's telling me. She's threatening me. What kind of paper would it be if every time one of the teachers doesn't like something, we have to pull it? What's the point of even having the paper then? The teachers might as well run it.

FRANK: Yeah, but you even said yourself the letter went too far, and it wasn't signed…wait a minute. Did you write it?

EMMA: Of course not.

FRANK: Why didn't you tell them that then? They think you did. Endle does, anyway.

EMMA: I didn't tell them because they were trying to turn that into the issue. And it's not.

FRANK: So what's the issue then?

EMMA: They didn't like what the letter said. It could have been signed by a hundred students, it could have been a petition. It had nothing to do with whether it was signed or not. And anyway, I didn't say I wrote it, I just didn't deny it. Let them think what they want.

FRANK: Maybe you just don't like getting told what to do.

EMMA: Excuse me?

FRANK: Well, c'mon, let's face it, you're not exactly used to taking orders. You're usually the one giving them.

EMMA: Do you think Winthrow is right? Do you think we should print a retraction?

FRANK: You were going to do it anyway.

EMMA: Do you think she should be able to tell us what goes in the student newspaper?

FRANK: Well, no, but…

EMMA: But what.

FRANK: You're just asking for trouble, Em.

EMMA: It's easy to stay out of trouble. Just go with the flow. But just because it's easy doesn't make it right.

Are you with me on this or not?

FRANK: Of course I am.

EMMA: Okay. Now the biggest obstacle we have is that the school provides most of the paper's budget, so they can exercise control whether we like it or not. So, what's the first thing we need?

Silence.

FRANK: Hmm? Are you asking me?

EMMA: Yes.

FRANK: Oh. Well...umm...money?

EMMA: Exactly. If we can make the paper financially autonomous, we don't have to answer to the school. So how do we do that?

FRANK: We...uh...autono what?

EMMA: Autonomous. Self-governing. Without help.

FRANK: Oh. We...you're still asking me, right?

EMMA: Yes.

FRANK: Okay. We...oh, wait. I know this. We do some fund-raising. Let everyone know what's happening. See if we can get services donated. Maybe somebody's whatever owns a paper store, that kind of thing.

EMMA: Exactly. Good thinking, Frank.

FRANK: I'm not just a pretty face, you know.

EMMA: Yeah. I can see that. Come on. We have a lot of work to do.

FRANK: Emma...

EMMA: What?

FRANK: Thanks.

EMMA: For what?

FRANK: For taking the rap for me. This whole thing was my fault. I was the one that didn't pull the letter.

EMMA: It's not about the letter anymore.

FRANK: Yeah, well, thanks anyway. It's…you know…it was nice…

FRANK is trying to make a move on EMMA.

EMMA: What are you doing?

FRANK: I just…I wanted to…nothing. Forget it. Just…thanks.

EMMA: You're welcome. C'mon.

EMMA exits, with FRANK shuffling behind her.

BULLETIN BOARD

An open letter,
Further to the letter published in the last edition of the Murphy High Review — I thought the author, who was too cowardly to stand behind his opinion, was way off base in his criticism of Mr. Endle. I for one find him to be consistently encouraging and supportive. Kudos to you, Mr. Endle. Keep up the good work.
Terrence Pereglio
P.S. Is it okay if I hand my Chem paper in late?

The school buzzer sounds.

Lights find FRANK, handing out flyers to the audience, in full protest mode.

FRANK: Stop the tyranny! Down with the oppressor! Stand up and be heard! We will not be the administration's doormat!

EMMA enters, pursuing FRANK.

EMMA: Frank…

FRANK: Sure it's just a newspaper, but what's next? Dress codes? Book burnings? Curfews? What is this, Russia?

EMMA: Frank!

FRANK: Hiya, Em. S'up?

EMMA: What are you doing?

FRANK: Drumming up support.

EMMA: Sounds like you're trying to start a riot.

FRANK: Ya gotta get the blood pumpin', you know? Get people excited.

EMMA: Your rally cry is a little dated.

FRANK: What do you mean?

EMMA: Russia's not a communist country anymore.

FRANK: No kidding. When did that happen?

EMMA: Oh, like years ago.

FRANK: I must've missed that class. Anyway, who cares? As long as it gets people riled up.

EMMA: If we're going to make our point, we have to keep this reasonable. We can't let it get out of hand.

FRANK: It's already out of hand, Emma. Way out of hand. We are the victims of an oppressive regime. We must stand up and fight! Our voices must be heard! Down with the fascist dictators! Down with the oligarchical pundits! We will overcome! We will overcome!

Silence. EMMA is staring at him.

EMMA: Oligarchical pundits?

FRANK: I have no idea what it means. I think I was channelling.

EMMA: I talked to Jennifer Mundy. Her dad owns a printing place. She thinks she can get him on board. And the donation jar in the cafeteria was already full from this morning.

MR. ENDLE approaches.

FRANK: Excellent. I've papered the school with the flyer. Everybody knows what's going on. They're all on our side. This should be a breeze.

MR. E: Emma. Just the person I wanted to see.

EMMA: Mr. Endle.

MR. E: I see you've been a busy young lady. The whole school is buzzing. Very clever of you.

EMMA: Thank you.

MR. E: I've written a letter to the editor I thought you might include in the first issue of the new paper. I have a copy of it here, if you'd like to give it a read.

           He hands her a letter. She begins to look it over.

MR. E: I thought it might be timely to do a little critique of how I think you're doing as student council president. In keeping with your proposed editorial policy of free speech.

           Is there something wrong, Emma?

EMMA: You can't seriously expect me to print this.

MR. E: I'm sorry. Have I misspelt something?

EMMA: Autocratic...self-serving...stubborn... Okay. I see what you're trying to do. But it's not the same thing.

MR. E: You're right. It's not the same thing. I'm willing to put my name to that. I'm not afraid to stand behind my words.

EMMA: I didn't write the letter, Mr. Endle. But even if I did, that's not the point.

MR. E: And the point is?

EMMA: You can't censor something just because you don't like it.

MR. E: But you're going to censor this letter, aren't you?

EMMA: That's...this is...this is different. You're just making this up to get back at me.

MR. E: I'm not trying to get back at you, Emma. I'm trying to make you see what you're doing.

EMMA: I see perfectly well what I'm doing. I'm standing up for the rights of the students.

MR. E: And what about the rights of the teachers?

EMMA: Teachers don't have…

Silence.

MR. E: Teachers don't have what? Rights?

EMMA: Of course they do. But it's not my responsibility to protect them.

MR. E: So a student has the right to criticise me in a school-funded paper, but I don't have the right to criticise a student in a student-funded paper.

EMMA: That's not what you really want. What you really want is to be protected. To be immune from criticism. It has nothing to do with "rights."

MR. E: That letter was slanderous, Ms. Hogan. As the editor of the paper, you could be held legally responsible. Do you understand that?

Perhaps that's a little beyond you. It doesn't matter anyway. Even if you manage to cover all the costs of the paper, we can still ban it from being on school property. You can't win this, Emma, but I am willing to meet you halfway. I will forgo an apology if you print this letter. Show me you really believe in a forum for free speech, and we'll let you have it.

I best get to class. Have a nice day.

MR. ENDLE leaves.

FRANK: Are you okay?

EMMA: It is different. Whoever wrote that letter criticising him wrote it because they believed in what they were saying. And it was the truth. Endle didn't write this because he believes I'm self-serving, or stubborn. He wrote it to force my hand. It is different, and it's not fair.

FRANK: It's okay. We'll figure it out.

EMMA: There's nothing to figure out. They run the school, they hold all the cards. So they're going to get what they want. It doesn't matter what we do. It's just not fair!

FRANK: Calm down, Em. It's not that big a deal.

EMMA: Yes, it is that big a deal! I can't back down now. The whole school knows what's going on. If I back down on this, if I let Endle and Winthrow get their way, if I wimp out, what do you think everyone is going to be calling me behind my back then?

FRANK goes to her, puts his arm around her.

FRANK: It's okay, Em, it's only as big a deal as you make it. It'll be fine…

She pulls away.

EMMA: What are you doing?

FRANK: I'm just trying to make you feel better…

EMMA: Well, don't!

Silence.

FRANK: Fine.

FRANK begins to leave.

EMMA: Frank…

FRANK: What?

EMMA: I'm sorry. I didn't mean that.

Silence.

FRANK: Oh…oh oh oh…wow. I think I've got an idea. Wow. This is really cool. I think I've got an idea. A good one.

EMMA: What?

FRANK: A web site.

EMMA: What?

FRANK: You're right. It's not fair. You shouldn't have to decide what should go in the paper. What should be printed and what should be left out. That's the part that's not fair, right?

EMMA: Yeah…

FRANK: So let's open it up. Let's start a school web site, instead of the paper. Make it a message board, like a chat room, so people can post whatever they want. It's easy enough to set up.

EMMA: Yeah, but…we have to have some control.

FRANK: Why?

EMMA: Well, because, it's…it's the school newspaper, and we're the editors. If we just throw it wide open…well…what are we editing?

FRANK: That's the whole point. We don't edit it. We set it up, and let 'er rip. If Mr. Endle wants to post his boring old letter, let him. If I want to do a swimsuit spread, why not? Isn't that what this is all about?

EMMA: What about school information? Schedules, and announcements / and…

FRANK: / All the boring stuff? We can still do that. But instead of letters to the editor, or the bulletin board page, we have an open message board. A free forum to say whatever you want. It's completely outside of the school's jurisdiction, there's nothing they can do about it, it's perfect. It's exactly what you've been talking about. Give it up. Whatever anybody wants to say, they say it. Total anarchy. Wow. I'm liking this. Is this a good idea or what?

EMMA: Yeah…

FRANK: I better watch myself. People are going to start expecting good marks and stuff. Em? What's wrong?

EMMA: I am such a hypocrite. You come up with a great idea that would take this whole thing out of my hands, into a free forum, where it belongs, and I can't stand that it might be out of my control. It makes me crazy.

FRANK: Okay, I'm not even sure what a hypocrite is, but if it's saying one thing and doing another, hey, welcome to the real world, oh perfect one. You're surrounded by hypocrates.

EMMA: Crites. Hypocrites.

FRANK: Crites, crates, whatever. The point is, the whole world is full of them. The trick is to know when you're doing it. Like right now, you know you're being a hypo whatever, hippopotamus, so just don't be one.

EMMA: It's not that simple…

FRANK: Yes, it is. Just give it up. Let it go. What's stopping you?

         Silence.

EMMA: Nothing. Nothing's stopping me. If I don't want to be a hippopotamus, I just won't be one. Right?

FRANK: So you want to start a web site?

EMMA: Yeah.

FRANK: Welcome to Fred's world. Where everything is completely out of your control.

         They exit.

MESSAGE BOARD

Congrats Murphy High on the new web site. It's about time you crawled out of the nineteenth century. See you at the Provincials, losers!
Yours in disdain, Ledley High.

MESSAGE BOARD

To: Marty in math class. I know you're stoned every day. I can tell. I'm watching you. Don't get paranoid or nothin', okay?

MESSAGE BOARD

To Rachel Cuddy from Amanda Dillan — did it ever occur to you that maybe W. was lying about N. to get back at me for C.B. asking me to the Halloween dance instead of her? If you were a real friend, you would have figured that out. I am so not your friend way more than you could ever not be mine. I wouldn't phone you if my hair was falling out and you had the only cure. So there.com.

    FRANK is at his computer. EMMA is lying on the floor, surrounded by books, working on a school assignment.

FRANK: So who do you figure W is? Wanda or Wendy?

EMMA: Must be Wanda. Wendy's too smart for that crowd.

FRANK: Lucky Wendy. Hey, I think there's some kind of porn link posted on here. You want to check it out?

EMMA: Of course not. Why would you think I'd want to do that?

FRANK: I don't know. For a laugh. See what's going on out there.

EMMA: You don't look at that stuff, do you?

FRANK: No. No way. I mean, not really. Well. Maybe sometimes. But just for a laugh. It's no big deal. Not like some of the guys. They live off the stuff.

EMMA: I just don't get that. What's the appeal?

FRANK: It gets 'em all horned up, I guess. Some of the guys, man, it's just stupid. They haven't had both hands free since puberty hit, if you know what I'm saying.

EMMA: Thank you, Frank, for that lovely image.

FRANK: Yeah, well, you know what I'm talkin' about.

EMMA: Unfortunately, yes, I do. Why anybody would find that garbage sexy is beyond me. Even the word sounds stupid. Porn. Sounds like some kind of fried meat. "I'll have some porn and a side of coleslaw." I can't think of a bigger turn-off.

FRANK: Yeah. Me too.

EMMA: Shouldn't you be working on your essay?

FRANK: I'm done already.

EMMA: No way. Let me see it.

FRANK: It's not written down yet. But it's done in my head.

EMMA: You can't hand your head in on Monday morning.

FRANK: Whatever.

EMMA: What are you focusing on?

FRANK: What do you mean what am I focusing on? We don't have a choice, do we?

EMMA: Of course we do. It's rituals in African tribal culture. That's a huge topic. There's lots of opportunities in there, ways you could make it more specific. If you just focus on one part of it, you'll learn way more.

FRANK: See, there's a few words I'd never use talking about an assignment. Opportunity. Focus. Learn.

EMMA: That's why you barely pass and I get A's.

FRANK: So what are you "focusing" on?

EMMA: A tribe in the Congo interior. I'm looking at their mating rituals. They've distilled the entire thing down to one dance, held once a year. See, the boys and the girls are separated from birth, and the most valuable commodity in this tribe is jewellery, which is passed down through the women, and the men aren't allowed to cut their hair, and once a year, they have this dance.

FRANK: What do you mean, like a rave or something?

EMMA: No, not a rave. Just a dance. And the women wear all their best jewellery and paint themselves all up, and the men braid their hair up all fancy and dance for the women. This is the only contact they're allowed, all year long.

FRANK: Get out.

EMMA: Yes. And if a woman is interested in a man, she jingles her jewellery, and if he's interested back, he flicks his hair at her. All the marriages are decided that day, right on the spot, and as soon as a couple gets married, the bride has to give all her jewellery away to her closest unmarried female relative, and the groom has to cut all his hair off.

FRANK: That's pretty freaky.

EMMA: The freaky part is nobody ever gets divorced. There's not even a word for it in their language.

     So, what are you doing?

FRANK: Ah, it's dumb.

EMMA: Maybe I can give you a hand.

FRANK: I just thought it might be fun to look at the way people our age go out with each other, but, like, look at it as if I belonged to one of those tribes in Africa? You know, like…I don't know…like the way the energy changes between two people if they like each other, the way it makes them move different, so if one person does something then the other one automatically adjusts, like their energy is attached or shared or something. There's something kinda real about it, you know? Kinda earthy. Something that's still connected to all that tribal stuff.

It's dumb, eh?

EMMA: I don't think it's dumb.

Silence.

FRANK: So you hear anything else from Winthrow, or Endle?

EMMA: No.

FRANK: Maybe they're okay with this. I mean, it hardly has anything to do with the school anymore. That's how it feels when you log on. It's just another glob of information floating around in space. Maybe they've forgotten all about it.

EMMA: I don't think Winthrow forgets about anything, and I know Endle doesn't. He didn't post the letter, I knew it was just a bluff, but he won't even look at me in Chem anymore.

FRANK: I couldn't stand that. Tension makes me nervous. I always feel like I gotta take a piss.

EMMA: Frank. Don't be a pig.

FRANK: What?

EMMA: Don't say piss.

FRANK: What am I supposed to say? Number one? Gimme a break. It's just a word.

EMMA: Say urinate. That's the proper name for it.

FRANK: Geez, you're weird sometimes.

EMMA: What?

FRANK: C'mon. Urinate? I gotta go urinate? Who talks like that?

EMMA: It's the proper name for it. Piss is made up. It's a colloquialism.

FRANK: A who's in the what now?

EMMA: It's like…I don't know…like all those words they used in
           the 60's. Like groovy, and hip. They're just made up words
           that a bunch of people shared for a while and then they
           disappeared.

FRANK: So what's wrong with that?

EMMA: It doesn't matter what you're thinking, it's no good if you
           can't communicate it. So why use words that people don't
           understand, or words that are going to disappear in a
           couple of years.

FRANK: Oh, come on. Everybody knows what piss means. It's not
           like a secret or something.

EMMA: Yeah, but in a couple of hundred years not everybody will
           know. And I bet urinate will still be around.

FRANK: Yeah, but like, who cares, 'cause I won't be. So in the
           meantime why not say piss.

EMMA: Because it's gross!

FRANK: See there it is. You're getting all proper and literate with
           your words and really you're just grossed out. Piss makes
           you picture it, so you don't want to use the word. Pisss.
           Pissssssss. I'm going to go take a pisssssssssss.

EMMA: Cut it out!

FRANK: Pisssssssssssssssssss.

EMMA: Urinate urinate urinate…

FRANK: Pisssssssssssssssssssss…

EMMA: Urinate urinate urinate!

           They both dissolve in laughter.

           Silence.

FRANK: That was weird.

EMMA: Yeah.

           Silence.

FRANK: So how come you still use books?

EMMA: What do you mean?

FRANK: You never use the Net for your homework and stuff. How come?

EMMA: I use it. But books are better for reading. You can lie down, or carry them around / with you.

FRANK: / Do you like me?

EMMA: Of course I like you. You've been my best friend since grade seven.

FRANK: Yeah, I know, but that's not what I mean. I mean, do you like me, do you think I'm, you know…

EMMA: You're creeping me out…

FRANK: It's not like I'm saying piss or something. I'm just asking if you like me.

EMMA: Do you like me?

Silence. EMMA gets up and goes to the computer, sits beside FRANK.

EMMA: Let's look up my tribe. Maybe I'm missing something.

FRANK: Okay.

EMMA takes the keyboard and begins a search.

Lights fade.

MESSAGE BOARD

Well. It would seem we don't have a lot of plant lovers at Murphy High. But that's all right. Our friends the flowers don't hold a grudge. Unfortunately, our friends the flowers aren't giving up their free time to organize this. So. We'll try one more time. The Horticulturist's Society will meet in Rm. #138 (that's the biology lab in case I wasn't clear about that in my last message), Friday at 4:00. I'm bringing home-made cookies and my prize hibiscus, so it'll be worth the trip. See you there.
Lisa Rebo.

MESSAGE BOARD

To anyone who cares —
So what's the fuss with Endle, the Chem teacher? So, what, he's like any more or less boring than any of the other ******* teachers in this *****-hole? I don't think so. They're all boring, and we can complain about it all we want, and nothing's going to change. Nobody gives a flying *****. Get over it.
Yours,
Zap.

INTERCOM ANNOUNCEMENT

Emma Hogan to the office, please. Emma Hogan to the office.

The school buzzer goes.

Ms. WINTHROW, in her office. She is at her computer screen.

EMMA enters.

EMMA: You wanted to see me?

Ms. W: Have a seat. Where is Fred?

EMMA: His name is…never mind. Is he supposed to be here? I can get him. I wouldn't mind a witness.

Ms. W: There's no need for that kind of tone. I'm glad he's not here. I wanted to talk with you privately.

EMMA: Look, Ms. Winthrow, let me save you some trouble here, okay? I admit that letter should have never been printed, but only because it wasn't signed. The paper is a forum for students to express their views, regardless of what they are. You oppose that. You think the teachers should be protected, immune to criticism.

Ms. W: Don't tell me what I think!

EMMA: You know what? It doesn't matter what you think anyway. It's not an issue anymore. There is no more paper. It's out of both of our hands. And you can thank yourself for that.

Ms. W: I've called you down to the office to discuss your suspension from school, Ms. Hogan.

Silence.

EMMA: What do you mean?

Ms. W: I've approached the school board. I'm going to have you suspended.

EMMA: You can't do that.

Ms. W: On the contrary. I have quite a good case. Your actions are jeopardising the well-being of the school, and I am taking the necessary steps to prevent that from happening.

EMMA: I haven't done anything wrong. You can't punish someone for opening a web site.

Ms. W: You're still calling it the Murphy High Review. You're characterizing it as a replacement for the school newspaper. It doesn't matter if it's not on school property, or if it's independent of school funding. You're identifying it as a school forum. Honestly. For someone who is so bright, your occasional naiveté amazes me.

EMMA: Ms. Winthrow. Please. My parents'll freak. I'll miss all my classes, student council, everything. I'll be humiliated in front of everybody. In front of the whole school. Please don't do this. We can work something out.

Ms. W: You're leaving me no other choice.

EMMA: Please…

Ms. W: I'm sorry.

Silence.

EMMA: I'm not naive, Ms. Winthrow. I'm not. An open message board? You think I don't know what's going to happen? The kind of things people are going to post? I'm one of the targets. I'm one of the ones they make fun of. But that doesn't give me the right to shut it down. I can't stop it just to protect myself. It's not fair to the people who are using it to say something decent, to express a real opinion, or to share an idea.

Ms. W: When you're older, Emma, you will understand that there is a big difference between allowing something and encouraging it.

EMMA: What are you so afraid of?

Ms. W: One does not have to be afraid to be wary, and I am extremely wary of any forum that breeds degeneracy and illiteracy, that allows wanton acts / of cruelty...

EMMA: / But if you disagree with it, or you don't like it, you can ignore it. Or post a reply. It's your choice. That's the whole point. It's a free forum. That's what scares you. I've taken away your control. I've upset the balance, and so now I have to be punished.

Ms. W: I think this meeting is over. Your student privileges, including the student council, are suspended as of tomorrow morning. I will let you know as soon as I've heard from the school board.

EMMA: Can I ask you something?

Ms. W: I would strongly suggest you don't push this any further, Ms. Hogan. You're not helping your situation.

EMMA: Please. I'd like to ask you one simple question. Please.

Ms. W: What?

EMMA: If over time the web site actually opens lines of communication, and it doesn't cause riots, and the school doesn't burn down, and the English language doesn't disintegrate into monosyllabic swear words and Neanderthal grunts, and time marches on and nobody but you and I even care if this ever happened, if it all just turns out okay, will you still think I've done something wrong?

Ms. W: Look, Emma, I am trying to maintain an environment where people can teach, and people can learn. How can that happen without respect? Mutual respect. How can that happen in an environment where students are openly criticizing teachers, and teachers are openly criticizing students, where there isn't even a basic respect for the language we share? It's deplorable. It's a mystery to me that someone with your intelligence and insight can't see what you and Fred are encouraging, what you're facilitating.

EMMA: His name is Frank. Not Fred. Frank. And it's a mystery to me how you can talk about respect, and not be able to remember a simple thing like that. Excuse me, Ms. Winthrow, I have to go take a piss.

EMMA exits. Lights fade on Ms. WINTHROW.

MESSAGE BOARD

To Amanda Dillan from Rachel Cuddy — C.B. asked you to the Halloween dance? Eewww! You never told me that! All is forgiven. Call me.

MESSAGE BOARD

To Amanda Dillan and Rachel Cuddy — Why do you think we care? Quit polluting the message board with your stupid little tiffs and gossip. You're just looking for attention. It's boring. W.
P.S. C.B. did NOT ask you to the Halloween dance, Amanda. That is such a lie.

MESSAGE BOARD

To all students and faculty.
Please take note that the Murphy High Horticulturist's Society is officially cancelled due to lack of interest. It has gone the way of the inflorescent houstonia longifolia gaerth, and we all know what that means. I hope you're all happy in your little barren concrete jungle hell.
Yours, Lisa Rebo.

FRANK is working at the computer, listening to music.

His DAD walks by.

DAD: *(shouting over the music)* How's the studying going?

FRANK: *(shouting back)* It's going okay!

DAD: Great!

FRANK: Hey, Dad! Can I talk to you about something?

DAD: Sure!

FRANK: It's kind of personal!

DAD: Maybe we shouldn't be shouting then!

FRANK: What?

DAD: Maybe you should turn down the music!

FRANK: What?

DAD: The music! Turn down the music!

FRANK: I can't hear you! Just a sec! I'll turn down the music!

          FRANK clicks off the computer.

          What did you say?

DAD: Nothing. What are you listening to?

FRANK: It's a radio download. That was Triple J, from Australia.
          There's lots of jazz junk, too, if you want to check it out.

DAD: Maybe later. What's on your mind? Are you in some kind
          of trouble? You pregnant?

FRANK: Dad! It's nothin' like that. I'm just feeling guilty 'cause I
          think Emma's in trouble / and...

DAD: / Emma's pregnant?

FRANK: No! Dad, you're not listenin', not that kind of trouble,
          trouble with Winthrow, and I'm feeling totally guilty about
          the whole thing, 'cause I think maybe it's my fault but it's
          not even about what it's really about anymore, it's gotten all
          blown out of proportion and it's about something entirely
          different now so I don't have a friggin' clue how to fix it,
          and Emma's not returning my calls or my e-mails and I
          haven't seen her at school and I'm kinda worried about
          her.

DAD: Is it your fault, or does it just feel like it's your fault because
          you're a good guy and you care about people?

FRANK: Dad.

DAD: What?

FRANK: You shouldn't say nice things right to a person's face. It's
          embarrassing. And yeah, it is my fault. I was supposed to

pull this stupid letter and I forgot, and Emma got in a big stand-off with Ms. W and then we started this web site and that was kind of my idea too…well, it was totally my idea, and then the web site got outta hand and Winthrow and Emma locked horns again and I think Emma lost, and I don't know what to do.

Silence.

Well?

DAD: What?

FRANK: What am I going to do?

DAD: I'm not going to tell you what to do.

FRANK: What do you mean you're not going to tell me what to do! You're my dad! This is where you're supposed to go "Well, son, the perfect thing to do right now would be to blah blah blah blah blah. Now off you go."

DAD: Do I sound like that?

FRANK: No, but you should. That's what dads are supposed to sound like.

DAD: I can't tell you what to do. I still don't have a friggin' clue what the problem is.

FRANK: How come Winthrow would make such a big deal out of a little bit of swearing? Everybody swears. They say shit on TV. How can she make such a big deal out of it?

DAD: Well, first of all, not everybody swears. A lot of people have a problem with it. Words have power. They can hurt people.

FRANK: Yeah, but if someone calls me a little shit, it's not the word that's hurting, it's what's behind it. You take away a person's weapon, they'll just find another weapon. It's the person that's the problem.

DAD: You're a pretty smart fella, François.

          Silence.

FRANK: Why did you call me that?

DAD: It's just a name, a word. Why do you care if I call you François?

                Silence.

FRANK: Because it has power.

DAD: Why does it have power?

FRANK: Because it's a stupid name.

DAD: You're the one who's decided it's stupid. You're the one that's making it a weapon.

FRANK: So then what's Winthrow's big problem with the swearing? She's treating it like a federal offence.

DAD: I don't know what the whole situation is, but I can guarantee you that it's not as simple as a bit of swearing. Nothing ever is.

FRANK: Yeah, well, I guess it's not just the swearing. It's the whole message board, the Net, all of it. All the garbage and crap, it's like it brings out the worst in people. It's like they screw around with it just 'cause they can, 'cause it's free and it's anonymous and they can be whoever they want and I guess a lot of people want to be assholes and dirtbags, and Winthrow doesn't like it, but she can't do anything about it so she's blaming Emma.

DAD: Of course Emma doesn't have anything to do with this.

FRANK: Well, sure she does. I mean, it's Emma. If she makes up her mind about something, you couldn't pay me to argue her down. I'd rather pull out my own teeth. But I still think it's Winthrow's fault way more than Emma's.

DAD: It doesn't have to be anybody's fault, Frank. Take the blame and the fault out of it. Then at least you have a chance of seeing how you can help. There's enough blame in the world already. We don't need to add to it. I don't mean that you're adding to it. That's not what I meant. I just think we need to be aware of it, you know? That's the first step to understanding. Awareness. Not that you're not aware already, I think that you're very / aware…

FRANK: / Dad?

DAD: Yeah…

FRANK: This is getting pretty boring.

DAD: Right. (*he heads for the computer*) Play me some jazz junk.

FRANK: What city do you want?

DAD: Montreal, s'il tu plait.

FRANK: Bon choix.

Funky jazz junk builds in.

MESSAGE BOARD

To: Frankie McBarrister. So why don't you just do that bitch Emma Hogan already. The whole school knows you want to. Maybe if you laid her the pipe she'd loosen up a bit, let you off the chain, whippin' boy.

Lights find Ms. WINTHROW, at a computer terminal, scanning the message board.

MESSAGE BOARD (cont'd)

And Winthrow, you hag, could you be any uglier? If you smiled, your head would probably crack open. Loosen the bone, Wilma. Lighten up. You're scaring the kids.
Zap.

P.S. You have shit for brains, and you smell like something died.

FRANK approaches Ms. WINTHROW's office. He stops and watches her.

FRANK: Ms. Winthrow?

Ms. W: Hmm? Yes. What can I do for you, Frank?

FRANK: It's…oh. Yeah. Frank. You got it right. Thanks.

Ms. W: It's nothing you need to thank me for. It's your name. I should know it.

FRANK: Are you okay?

Ms. W: I was just reading the message board.

FRANK: Don't let it get to you. It's mostly that Zap guy, whoever he is. Just some loser looking for a life. I don't think you're a hag.

Ms. W: Yes, well, thank you. What can I do for you?

FRANK: I have an idea for the web site. I wanted to talk to you about it.

Ms. W: I think we've all had enough of the web site, Frank. It would be best if we left that particular topic alone.

FRANK: I know what you're afraid of. I think I can fix it.

Ms. W: Pardon me?

FRANK: I mean…well, not afraid, but what's bugging you. About Emma, and the web site. See, you and Emma, you're an awful lot alike, and what Emma didn't like about it was she had no control over it, and when Emma doesn't have control over something it makes her all nervous and antsy 'cause she's smart and she usually knows how things should be done and when she doesn't have control over something she gets all nervous 'cause it might not get done the right way. And if it doesn't get done the right way she thinks people will think less of her, 'cause she's really pretty insecure and she wants people to like her, and she thinks people will like her more if everything she does is perfect, you know? And, well, you two are kind of the same that way, so I thought maybe I could fix the web site so you wouldn't have to be so uptight about it. Not uptight. I don't mean uptight like uptight, I mean uptight like insecure. So you wouldn't have to be so insecure about it.

Silence.

Okay, that all sounded like some big insult and I didn't mean it to at all. I meant it like a good thing. It's okay to be uptight and insecure about stuff. I'm insecure about just about everything, I mean like right now I'm so insecure that if you don't say something pretty soon I think I might like puke or something?

Ms. W: What's your idea?

FRANK: Well, see, right now it's an anonymous post, a message board, anybody can log on and enter anything they want, like a chat room, so I was thinking what if they had to enter their student numbers with a password to log on to the site, and that way if somebody writes something that maybe they shouldn't have, you could trace it back to them with their student number, and that way you'd still have control, right?

Ms. W: If I didn't like what someone was saying, I could shut them down.

FRANK: Yeah, yeah, exactly. You could weed out the Zaps. And if you had control again, then maybe, you know, maybe…

Ms. W: Everything would be all right with Emma.

FRANK: She didn't want it to go this far. She just gets stuck on stuff, 'cause she wants to do the right thing.

Ms. W: I'm just trying to do the right thing too. She's lucky to have a friend like you.

FRANK: She doesn't know I'm here. She'd kill me if she knew I was talking to you about this.

Ms. W: I won't tell her.

FRANK: So are we okay here? Should I fix the site?

Ms. W: Tell me something, Frank. That horrid message, about you and Emma…

FRANK: …Yeah…

Ms. W: …how did that make you feel?

          Silence.

FRANK: It made me mad.

Ms. W: Why?

FRANK: Because I didn't like the way he was talkin' about her.

Ms. W: But you still defend the web site.

FRANK: It's not the web site's fault. The web site is no different than the stupid letter that started this whole thing. It's just a message. The problem is the person writing the message.

          Silence.

Ms. W: Thanks for stopping by, Frank. I appreciate it.

FRANK: What about Emma?

Ms. W: That's between Emma and me.

            FRANK is about to leave. He stops.

FRANK: You know something, Ms. W? Maybe I shouldn't say this, but Mr. E really isn't a very good teacher. I know this isn't about that letter anymore, but I think it's important that you know that. We've got lots of good teachers, but we've got lots of bad ones, too, and he's definitely one of them, and we don't have any place to talk about it 'cause we're afraid we'll get flunked or something. That's why whoever wrote that letter didn't sign it.

Ms. W: I know.

FRANK: Am I in trouble for saying that?

Ms. W: No.

FRANK: Thanks.

            I better go. I must be late for something.

            FRANK leaves.

MESSAGE BOARD

To Amanda, Rachel and W.
From C.B.
Are you all insane? Why do you think I'd be interested in any of you? I'd rather sleep with a gibbon.

MESSAGE BOARD

To anybody who cares,
Just a reminder that the Murphy High Horticultural Society is cancelled. You could beg me to keep it going, and it would do no good. If you wanted to try, I'll be in Rm. #138 (that's the biology lab at the south end of the school, just down the hall from the library), at 4:00 on Wednesday the 16th, but really, you shouldn't bother, because I've made up my mind. I won't be expecting anybody.
Lisa Rebo.

MESSAGE BOARD

To C.B.

From W., Amanda and Rachel—

Just wanted to let you know that we know what a gibbon is, we looked it up, and we all agree that it's the only thing that would sleep with you, and as far as we're concerned you don't even exist anymore. So there.com.

EMMA is found, walking to class. FRANK runs after her.

FRANK: Emma! Wait up…

EMMA: Hey, you.

FRANK: Where are you going in such a hurry?

EMMA: Student Council meeting.

FRANK: No way! That's great! So you and Winthrow got everything worked out?

EMMA: We managed to get through a couple of meetings. You know, she's really not all that bad once you get to know her a bit.

FRANK: Really.

EMMA: Yeah. Things are still pretty tense with Endle, but that's only one class, I can handle that.

FRANK: What's going to happen with the web site?

EMMA: We'll redo the home page. Make sure it's clear the administration doesn't have anything to do with it. Past that, there's nothing much we can do.

FRANK: What about that Zap guy?

EMMA: If we shut it down, he'll just take his garbage somewhere else. I'd rather know what he's saying, thank you very much. That whole ignorance is bliss thing is way overrated.

FRANK: And you and Winthrow figured this all out.

EMMA: Yeah.

FRANK: The two of you.

EMMA: Yeah, so?

FRANK: Nothing.

EMMA: What?

FRANK: Nothing!

EMMA: We're working together to find a common solution.

FRANK: Good on ya.

EMMA: It's called being an adult, Frank.

FRANK: Absolutely.

EMMA: What are you smiling about?

FRANK: Nothin'. Can I take you out for lunch after your meeting?

EMMA: Why?

FRANK: What do you mean why. I gotta have a reason?

EMMA: You never take me out for lunch. Sounds like a date or something.

FRANK: Well, maybe it is a date. Yeah. It's a date. I like you, and I want to take you out on a date. A lunch date. So?

EMMA: So what?

FRANK: So you want to go for lunch or not?

EMMA: Yeah, sure, I guess.

FRANK: You don't have to sound so excited about it.

EMMA: What? You want me to start jingling my jewelry?

FRANK: No, but…you know…ah, forget it. I'll see you later.

He begins to leave. EMMA stops him.

EMMA: Hey.

FRANK: What?

EMMA kisses him.

EMMA: I'd like to go for lunch with you.

FRANK: That's…uh…yeah. Good. Good.

EMMA: C'mon. Walk me to my meeting.

EMMA heads off to her meeting, FRANK shuffling conspicuously behind her.

MESSAGE BOARD

Hi everyone. I'm new to the school, and I'm looking for fellow plant lovers. Is there anyone out there who is interested in horticulture? If there is, please post a reply, or e-mail me at greenthumb@hotmail.com. Looking forward to hearing from you.
Alexander Mortimer.

Blackout.

The End

First Production

The first production of *To Be Frank* was in the fall and winter of 2006, by Geordie Productions (Montreal, QC) as part of their seasonal school tour (Eastern and Northern Canada).

Director	Dean Patrick Fleming
Designer	Jeremy Gordaneer
Stage Manager	Stephane Rousseau

Frank	Danny Coleman
Emma	Kathleen Stavert
Ms. Winthrow	Anthousa Harris
Mr. Endle / Dad	Gino Durante

Acknowledgements

Much thanks to Iris Turcott (Factory Theatre) for her dramaturgical support, Paula Danckert and Rachel Hennessey (Banff playRites Colony) for their insights, K.C. (Clunage) for hers, and Leslie Silverman (Manitoba Theatre for Young People) for her support and feedback.

Written with the assistance of the Manitoba Arts Council and the 2001 Banff playRites Colony.

About the Playwright

Brian Drader is an actor, writer, dramaturge and artistic administrator whose plays have been produced in Canada, the United States, and Europe. Awards include the Herman Voaden National Playwriting Award, the Philadelphia Brick Playhouse New Play Award, Lambda Literary Award for Drama, finalist for the Governor General's award, the McNally Robinson Book of the Year, and the Joyce Dutka Arts Foundation Playwriting Competition, New York. His short film, *Iris And Nathan*, won the National Screen Institute Drama Prize. Two feature films, *The Return Of The Fabulous Seven* and *Please Mr. Please*, are currently in development. Brian's most recent play, *Curtsy*, was published by Signature Editions and *The Norbals, PROK* and *Liar* are all published by Scirocco Drama. Brian has also acted in over seventy professional theatre productions across Canada, as well as numerous films, television projects, and radio dramas. He is presently the Director of Playwriting for the National Theatre School of Canada in Montreal.

Interview

To Be Frank started its life in the year 2000, supported by a grant from the Manitoba Arts Council. I tackled a first draft which was then accepted at the Banff playRites Colony, 2001, where I had the good fortune to work with both Paula Danckert and Rachel Hennessey as dramaturgical support through a full rewrite and two readings. My long-time dramaturgical anchor and friend, Iris Turcott, got her hands on it after that, whipped it and me into shape, and with some invaluable feedback from Leslie Silverman (Manitoba Theatre for Young People) and my dear friend Kathy Clune, it landed, by 2003, in a draft that was very close to what it is today.

My inspiration for the play was twofold. First and foremost, the character of Emma is an investigation into what it is to be a teenage girl who is really, really smart and really, really driven, and the challenges a young person like that faces in a socio-demographic (high school) that is more inclined to reward those who are concerned and in tune with the social skills required to flourish in that unforgiving environment. At the time I had two nieces in high school, and a goddaughter, and I watched what they had to go through to survive, and as a gay male who had to survive my own trials and tribulations in high school, I felt for them every step of the way, and I wanted to protect them. I couldn't do that of course. I would have caused far more harm than good if I'd started accompanying them to classes. But I could write a play, and in my own way, maybe I could shed some light on that world.

I was also fascinated with all the new technology we were being bombarded with in the early 2000's. E-mail was certainly well imbedded in our culture, although still somewhat foreign to the older generations, but the Net itself was exploding. Communication as we knew it was changing dramatically. I found it fascinating and more than a little bit terrifying. I saw quite clearly the darker side of cell phones and emails and blogs that were distancing us from each other in the very act of trying to bring us all closer together. I'm not against these technologies, but I use them with caution. I value a lunch with someone infinitely more than a year of e-mail contact.

It was from this rumination that the idea came, the magic "what if" — what if the students in a high school used cyberspace, that deliciously anarchistic new frontier of free speech, to put their own school and its teaching body under the microscope?

The story really took off for me when I discovered Frank. Frank is who I think I used to be (except for the gay/straight thing). Maybe he is, or maybe he's just a false memory of who I was, or maybe just a part of who I was. What matters is that I very comfortably lived in his skin, and he came to me in torrents of monologues and thoughts and feelings that I could barely contain. The first big massive monologue in the play came to me in one sitting, almost in real time. Frank was Frank from the get-go.

And discovering Frank led to the final glue for the play, for me, and it seems this is always my final glue—I found my love story. Frank and Emma. I believe that in fictional story time and space, their children and grandchildren are gathering around them somewhere to celebrate their 50th wedding anniversary.

I didn't consciously set out to write a "play for young audiences." I set out to write a play for my nieces, and for my goddaughter, and soon enough for myself. Other people told me it was a TYA play. And of course it is. That's the audience. And I do believe it's a very smart thing to know who the audience is for a play that you're writing. Why not? I come from the personal school that says there is no end to what a storyteller should know about his or her story, and that includes how his or her story is landing with an audience. But honestly? I really wasn't setting out to write a TYA play. Once I realized that's what I was writing, things did change. The very simple fact is that in this country, the model for TYA touring and production is pretty entrenched, and pretty limited. I offer that as a generalization; most of the TYA theatres in the country do main-stage shows, which release them from the constraints of a touring production. But budgets are tight, and the tour (taking the play to the schools) still rules the roost. And that roost generally calls for a play that can be done by four actors and can start right after lunch and wrap up before that 2:00 bell announces the class change. Four actors, and just a minute or two under one hour. That, for better or for worse, is TYA in Canada. So my task became one of storytelling economy, to contain the play in terms of running time. As well, I had always conceived of the story as having five characters, so my concession there was to structure it in a way that the same actor could play both Dad and Mr. Endle.

In terms of the audience, once Frank and Emma came fully to life for me, and particularly when I discovered that Frank had a direct address with them, I no longer needed to worry about an age-appropriate tone or content. My sole task was to stay true to who Emma and Frank were, and the rest took care of itself.

I find it interesting that where I did need to be conscious that it was a play for teen audiences was with the older characters; Ms. Winthrow, Mr. Endle, and the dad. It was quite a balancing act to find the fulcrum between cartoon and fully fleshed out adults for all three. I unapologetically acknowledge that I have "pitched" both Mr. Endle and Dad a little towards the cartoon end of things. It's partly a style choice, but it's also being conscious of the audience for this play and what will make a satisfying story for them. Dad has a real heart and is trying to help his son, but he's flawed and a bit of a goof, and Mr. Endle, although he has an opportunity to share his point of view, is our barely three-dimensional villain. In my experience with this story in production, the teenagers love to hate Endle and they love to laugh at Dad. They serve their function. And paired — i.e. played by one actor — the two characters take on an interesting, larger dimension that neither inhabits individually.

I wanted Ms. Winthrow to be more than that. She needed to be a worthy foil for Emma, and indeed one of the things I enjoyed most in writing this play was discovering how much Ms. Winthrow and Emma had in common, and how that both complicated and abetted their journey.

Elsa Bolam, the founder of Geordie Theatre in Montreal, was the first to take a serious interest in the play. At the time there was a big news story about a controversial California web site, www.ratemyteachers.com that kids all across North America were logging on to. Schools were shutting down local access to the site, parents were in an uproar, teachers were livid with fear disguised as outrage, and the students were in anarchistic heaven. It seemed to be the right time for this play, but unfortunately Elsa wasn't able to find a place for it in her programming. But the year she retired she passed it by the incoming Artistic Director, Dean Fleming, who picked it up for their Eastern Canadian touring show. And what a great production it was, directed by Dean. It was everything that I hoped it would be, and more. A teen audience is such a glorious thing, as is any young audience. They're vocal. They feed back. They groan and laugh and gasp in ways that are so immediate and unfiltered. They haven't been trained into polite submission like adult audiences have. Watching *To Be Frank* with high school audiences was and is, to this day, the most satisfying playwright's experience I have ever had. Waiting with anticipation for the collective "wwwwooooooo!" when Emma asks Ms. Winthrow what she's so afraid of. Hearing the girls all giggle and watching the guys elbow each other when they realize Frank has a crush on Emma. And of course, the kiss. Love it. It's so intensely gratifying to know your play works because you can hear and see it work.

After a very successful run with Geordie I submitted *To Be Frank* to a yearly competition set up between the German and Canadian consulates. You submit your play, it's read by a panel of agents and theatre professionals, and if selected it's then represented by an agency in Berlin. The submission was successful, the play was translated into German, and in the 2008/2009 season it had a tremendously successful run at a theatre in Magdeburg. At the time of this publication, that production is transferring to Theatre Potsdam to open their 2009/2010 season, and another production of the play will be going up at the Theatre Baden-Baden. I have not had an opportunity (yet) to see a production of the play in German (I can only imagine what Frank's rambling opening monologue would sound like), but I did receive production photos from the Magdeburg show, and I was enthralled to see that indeed it was my play. There was Frank, and Emma, and Frank's dad, and Ms. Winthrow, and Mr. Endle, and I could recognize all of them, and even the set looked like the right set. How intensely satisfying to know that this story that I wrote for my nieces and my goddaughter was very much alive in another language in another country on the other side of this crazy planet we live on. That's why I write.

Binti's Journey

adapted by Marcia Johnson

from the novel *The Heaven Shop*
by Deborah Ellis

Characters

BINTI — adolescent girl, star of a radio drama
JUNIE — her older sister, engaged to be married
KWASI — the middle brother, loves to draw
MEMORY — adolescent girl, dislikes Binti at first
GOGO — grandmother to the three siblings, strong
Mr. WAJIRU — radio drama director
STEWART — adolescent boy, actor in a radio drama
REPORTER — woman
JEREMIAH — late teens, peer counselor
MACHOZI — rambunctious little girl
MARY — young, spiteful cousin to the siblings
OLD WOMEN
BOY
PASTORS
UNCLES
AUNTS
CHILDREN

Playwright's Notes

The original production of *Binti's Journey* was done with four actors but it is possible to have a larger or smaller cast. Gogo was played to great effect by three actors speaking in unison.

Key double casting in the original production was as follows:

Junie:	Mr. Wajiru, Machozi
Memory:	Mary, Reporter
Kwasi:	Stewart, Jeremiah, Boy

Other minor characters such as pastors, children and old women were played in unison or divided amongst the cast.

Prologue

Music/Movement overture which culminates in an ensemble image of Gogo's family.

They break out of the pose and greet the audience.

ALL: Nda. [pr. nn-DAH]

BINTI: This is my sister, Junie; *(JUNIE waves);* my brother Kwasi [pr.KWA-cee] and this is—

MEMORY: Memory.

BINTI: Our cousin. *(BINTI holds up the newspaper)* And this was me one year ago: Binti Phiri, star of Malawi's most popular radio show. I don't even recognize that girl anymore.

So much has happened since then…to all of us. So much has changed. Especially me.

BINTI stands in front of her microphone.

Scene 1 — Recording Studio

BINTI: Your mother died of AIDS.

STEWART: She did not.

BINTI: She did, too. Everyone knows it.

WAJIRU: Cut!

STEWART: She died. She just died. She didn't have AIDS.

BINTI: She was a bad woman…

WAJIRU: Cut!

BINTI: …and she died of AIDS and…

WAJIRU: Binti!

BINTI finally hears him and stops.

WAJIRU: You are not holding yourself at the proper distance from the microphone.

BINTI: Yes, Mr. Wajiru. *(to MEMORY)* We were rehearsing for a special anniversary episode of *Gogo's Family*. It was going to be recorded at the Mount Soche Hotel. Mr. Wajiru wanted us to be perfect.

STEWART sticks his tongue out at BINTI.

BINTI: *(so WAJIRU can't hear)* Your part is so easy a chicken could play it.

WAJIRU: As for the rest of you, you could all take a lesson from the way Binti was reading that scene. She sounded like an actual person.

BINTI gloats in STEWART's direction.

WAJIRU: *(catching BINTI)* Now, if she could just sound like an actual person into her microphone.

BINTI: *(deflating)* Yes, Mr. Wajiru.

WAJIRU: Good. We will now take a break. Refresh yourselves. Binti, this is the journalist from the *Youth Times.*

MEMORY enters as REPORTER. WAJIRU exits.

REPORTER: Thank you for making the time to meet with me.

THEY shake hands. WAJIRU exits.

BINTI: *(to audience)* She talked to me like I was an adult! *(to REPORTER)* You're welcome.

REPORTER: Now I know you don't have a lot of time, so why don't we begin?

BINTI: All right.

REPORTER: Let's see, you are in standard seven at St. Peter's School for Girls; and a prefect at that! You're thirteen years old and your role on *Gogo's Family* is your first professional acting job.

BINTI: How do you know all this?

REPORTER: Tell me about *your* family.

BINTI: I live with my father, my sister Junie and my brother Kwasi. My mother died six years ago.

REPORTER: I see. What does your father do?

BINTI: Bambo makes and sells coffins. *(slowing down as if to give REPORTER a chance to write)* It's called Heaven Shop Coffins along New Chileka Road. *(back to normal)* We live in the back. Bambo's teaching carpentry to Kwasi and me, but we're not very good yet. I'm better than Kwasi, though.

REPORTER: Do you have a Gogo in your real life?

BINTI: My father's mother is the person I call Gogo. She lives in Mulanje. I never met my mother's mother.

REPORTER: Your voice is heard by millions of people every week, in homes and villages all over the country. I understand you get fan mail.

BINTI: Yes. I get lots of letters, from children and from grown-ups.

REPORTER: And what do they say?

BINTI: A lot of them tell me I'm being horrible. They think they are writing to Kettie, my character. The ones who write to me, Binti, say nice things, or they write about how something similar happened to them.

REPORTER: Tell me how you got the job.

BINTI: I had to audition. There was a long line-up of kids. We had to read something in front of adults. We were asked to do it again and again until I was the only one left. So they gave me the job!

REPORTER: Good for you. Now, *Gogo's Family* deals with serious issues like AIDS, crime, people losing their jobs. Do you always understand what is being talked about?

BINTI: Of course I understand. I'm very smart, or I wouldn't have gotten the job... *(to audience)* ...is what I wanted to say, but I didn't want the newspaper readers to think I thought too much of myself. What I really said was: *(to REPORTER)* Well, I try to act like a regular child would. In today's show, I make fun of a cousin who comes to live in our house. I don't want him to be there, so I try to make him feel bad by saying his mother died of AIDS. My character wants to make him feel ashamed. Kids will say things like that.

WAJIRU enters.

WAJIRU: *(to* REPORTER*)* I'm sure you have enough for your article. Go out to the front office. They'll give you some papers that will explain all that we are doing here. Storytime also publishes comic books on HIV/AIDS, nutrition and all sorts of things.

> REPORTER *reluctantly exits.* STEWART *enters. He and* BINTI *take their positions.*

WAJIRU: Is everybody here? Everyone in position? Good. Let's rehearse something that Malawi will find worth listening to.

BINTI: Your mother died of AIDS!

STEWART: She did not!

BINTI: She did, too. Everyone knows it…

> *Music transition.*

Scene 2 — Street and Phiri House

BINTI: *(to audience)* Blantyre is a busy city with paved streets and fancy bank buildings and I loved living there. On taping days, I was allowed to walk home from the radio house by myself. I liked holding my script like this; with the title page facing out so everyone could see it.

I loved being around all the shops, although I wasn't as big on shopping as Junie was. She would search through second-hand clothing stalls on New Chileka Road. Jeans, shirts, dresses and sweaters that people from America don't want anymore.

KWASI: Junie can spot something great in the middle of a large pile of ugly things.

BINTI: She wasn't in any of the stalls the day I'd had my interview with the reporter.

She was in the library with her fiancé, Noel. I saw them through the window and was just about to get their attention.

But I didn't want to interrupt two people who were crazy in love and hopeful for the future.

Kwasi enters, sits and sketches as though from a model.

BINTI: When I got home, Kwasi was sitting on the ground, leaning against a signpost.

KWASI: My fingers get hungry to draw.

BINTI: Birds are his specialty. He would draw one inside the bottom of every coffin.

KWASI: To help people fly faster to heaven.

BINTI: Today, he was drawing a picture of Bambo making a coffin.

BINTI looks at the picture KWASI is drawing.

BINTI: That's good, but you made him look too skinny.

KWASI: He *is* really skinny.

BINTI: Not *that* skinny. And you should slip some cardboard under your seat if you don't want Junie to nag you about dirt on your trousers.

KWASI: You're in my light.

He pushes BINTI out of the way and continues to draw.

Scene 3 — Outside Phiri House; on the way to school

BINTI: A few weeks later, Junie and I were getting ready for school.

JUNIE: Go put on your sweater.

BINTI: I was just opening the door to get it. It was light blue and went perfectly with my school uniform. But I don't like when Junie orders me to do things.

BINTI takes a stubborn stance.

JUNIE: Don't wear it then, but don't complain when you catch a cold and lose your voice and can't go on the radio.

JUNIE starts walking. BINTI follows.

BINTI: Why are you in such a bad mood?

JUNIE: I got up early to do the books.

BINTI: Was there something wrong?

JUNIE: There was a lot less money than there should have been. Bambo has given most of the profits from last month to the cousins. Any time we start to get ahead, he sends money off to the cousins. I know they're family, but how much money do they need? I asked him about it at breakfast.

BINTI: What did he say?

JUNIE: He said what he always says: "Don't you have food on your plate? Don't you sleep under a roof?" That's not everything. I'm going to say to him one of these days: "There's more to life than just eating and sleeping. There's thinking about the future, and planning for it."

BINTI: Is there something you need? I'm earning money.

JUNIE: Don't start talking to me about what a big star you are. This isn't about you.

BINTI: I only said...

JUNIE: You're just a child. You think that because today is wonderful, tomorrow will be wonderful, too. But it doesn't always work that way. Things go wrong. People get sick. We should be planning for when things don't go well. We should be putting money aside. That's what I learned in business class, but he gives it all away. "Family," he says, but what are we?

BINTI: Why wouldn't things go well?

JUNIE: Oh, back off, or you'll be in such trouble!

            JUNIE exits. Wind whips up. BINTI begins to shudder.

Scene 4 — Mount Soche Hotel/Hospital

            STEWART enters. He and BINTI take their positions.

BINTI: It was the six-month anniversary of *Gogo's Family*. The restaurant at the Meridian Mount Soche Hotel was turned into a radio studio for the special recording. I was wearing a dress made of chintje cloth. My stomach was all fluttery. Bambo, Kwasi and Junie were in the audience! Then, Stewart had to open his big mouth.

STEWART: Your father looks like he has the Slim.

BINTI: Shut up, donkey!

MEMORY: *(to audience)* The Slim is what some people call AIDS.

STEWART: Well, he looks just like my uncle before he died.

BINTI: Shut up! *(ENSEMBLE applauds; to audience)* We bowed for the audience, then did the taping.

V/O: And now it's time for *Gogo's Family.*

Music.

JUNIE: There was a dinner party after the show. Mr. Wajiru came over to say hello to the family.

BINTI: He and Bambo talked about football and politics. Then Mr. Wajiru asked to borrow me for a moment. He told me that I should take Bambo home. He said that Bambo was very sick and was only staying so that he wouldn't spoil my evening. So I pretended that I wanted to go home.

Music: BINTI and ENSEMBLE sadly walk home.

KWASI: Bambo got weaker and weaker.

JUNIE: He couldn't build coffins anymore.

BINTI: Our neighbour, Mr. Tsaka, had a new coffin shop.

KWASI: He got all Bambo's business.

BINTI: Unfortunately, the coffin business is booming in Blantyre.

When Bambo was too sick to get out of bed anymore, Junie, Kwasi and I took turns looking after him. One day, when it was my turn, Mr. Tsaka came for a visit. When he saw how sick Bambo was, he drove us to the hospital. There were so many people in line. I thought we could go to the front because Bambo was so sick. But so was everyone else. Mr. Tsaka had to leave. I sat on the floor and he rested Bambo's head on my lap.

We waited and waited. Finally, some men carried Bambo to a ward and a doctor examined him. *(to DOCTOR)* You don't have to check him for AIDS. Someone said that he has AIDS, but I'm sure he doesn't.

> *DOCTOR exits.*

BINTI: She checked his blood anyway. We had to wait.

The doctor said Bambo had pneumonia and gave me a bottle of pills. She said that we would know soon if he was strong enough to fight the pneumonia.

There were so many beds crowded together. They were all full. The men put Bambo on a mattress on the floor. I held Bambo's hand. He smiled and asked me to read the *Gogo's Family* script to him. When the other patients and their families heard me, they asked me to read louder so that everyone could hear. I did all the voices. It was fun. I did Stewart's part much better than he ever did. Bambo was so proud.

JUNIE: Later, Mr. Tsaka drove Kwasi and me to the hospital.

KWASI: A preacher visited the patients. He sang a song of prayer and praise, clapping a hand against his Bible to keep time.

> *Music. ENSEMBLE sings and dances. BINTI sways with the music. The singing underscores the following.*

BINTI: I knew that Bambo would get better and we would all be home together. He seemed better. He was going to get better.

But while everyone was singing and dancing, he…

> *Singing stops.*

ENSEMBLE: Binti. Look.

> *BINTI looks at the spot on the floor where Bambo lies. She realizes that he is gone.*

Scene 5 — Phiri House/Tsaka Coffin Yard/Funeral

JUNIE: Aunts, uncles and adult cousins came from far away after Bambo died.

BINTI:	Stealing everything from us; making us cook for them and clean up after them. Junie did whatever they said.

Kwasi enters, determined.

BINTI:	Kwasi, what are you doing?
KWASI:	I'm building a coffin for Bambo.
BINTI:	You?
KWASI:	He needs one and I am going to build him one.
BINTI:	But, you're no good at it and neither am I.
KWASI:	I just wasn't trying very hard before. If I try harder, I can build one, a good one. So, that's what I'm going to do.

Kwasi picks up a saw and begins to work.

BINTI:	One of the uncles stopped him.

Uncle puts his hand on Kwasi's.

UNCLE:	We don't want any of those boards sawed up. They are worth money and you don't know what you're doing.
KWASI:	Yes, I do.
UNCLE:	You are a schoolboy, not a working boy.

Uncle takes the saw from Kwasi's hand. Kwasi is devastated.

BINTI:	*(to Kwasi)* Come on. I have an idea.
KWASI:	She got her radio money.
JUNIE:	Kwasi and Binti went to Mr. Tsaka's coffin yard.
BINTI:	Mr. Tsaka's ready-to-assemble coffins didn't need the work of a skilled carpenter like Bambo.
KWASI:	But it was the best that we could do.
BINTI:	Mr. Tsaka would only take some of our money and told us to keep the rest of it safe and hidden. He drove us to the mortuary to get Bambo's body and then to the funeral.

Music.

ENSEMBLE moves to the funeral. GOGO enters.

BINTI: At the church, I saw an old woman walking down the aisle with the support of a young man. *(to JUNIE)* Junie, who's that?

JUNIE: You don't remember? That's Gogo.

BINTI: Gogo walked right up to the front of the church. She stood in front of the coffin.

GOGO: Open it up. I want to see my boy. Help me to see my boy or leave me alone.

The coffin is opened.

GOGO: That's him. That's my son. My young friend Jeremiah and I have just come from the hospital. The doctor told me there was AIDS in my boy's blood. He is the second son I have lost to AIDS. I have lost three daughters, too. All to the same thing. All to this AIDS. We do not want to say what it is. We think that if we don't say it, it will go away, but it won't go away.

           In the old days, when there were still lions around, if a lion came into our village and carried away our young, we did not keep silent! If we were silent, it would keep eating our children. We had to make noise. We had to bang pots and yell… There's a lion in the village.

           There is a lion in the village now. It is called AIDS and it is carrying away our children.

           So I want to say today, in front of all of you, that my son died of AIDS, and I loved him. His wife probably died of AIDS before him, and I loved her, too. And I am tired of burying my children.

KWASI: Gogo hugged us before going back to Mulanje with her friend Jeremiah.

ENSEMBLE: There's a lion in the village!

BINTI: *(to herself)* There's a lion in the village.

Scene 6 — Phiri House

BINTI and JUNIE are in bed.

BINTI: Junie, did Bambo really have AIDS?

JUNIE: He had pneumonia.

BINTI: But Gogo said…

JUNIE: Gogo is an old woman, and she was upset. Maybe she heard something at the hospital, maybe she didn't. If people ask, you tell them our father died of pneumonia.

BINTI: And Mama?

JUNIE: You tell them Mama died of TB. That's what I remember, and I was older than you and Kwasi when she died, so I remember best.

JUNIE lies down, preparing for sleep. BINTI listens for a moment, then nudges JUNIE.

BINTI: Junie! Do you hear them? They want to take us all out of school and live with them. They want to split us up!

JUNIE: What!

They listen for a moment to muffled voices.

JUNIE: Don't worry. I'll talk to them in the morning.

Scene 7 — Phiri House

JUNIE and BINTI speak to UNCLE and AUNT.

JUNIE: Uncle, we thank you for your concern.

UNCLE: Your father was our brother.

JUNIE: He would want us to stay together.

UNCLE: None of us can take all three of you. We all have our own families to take care of.

JUNIE: We own this house and we know that we cannot run the coffin business but we can rent it out to someone else who would like to run it and we can ask our pastor if there is a respectable person who could rent Bambo's room. Binti

and Kwasi can switch to a free school at the end of the
month when their fees run out.

I will stay at St. Peter's since it is my last year. Plus, I will
earn more money later on if I graduate. Kwasi will take on
a job at the market. So we will get by.

UNCLE: Your plan is good but you are mistaken about many things.
            For one thing, you do not own this house—

UNCLE & AUNT: We do.

UNCLE: We are the responsible adults, and your father's property
            comes to us. The house and the business are being sold. This
            is a good location, and we have already found a buyer.

JUNIE: But the money from the house...

UNCLE & AUNT: Will come to us.

UNCLE: We are responsible for your care.

JUNIE: I understand, Uncle, but—

UNCLE: We have obtained a refund from your schools.

AUNT: Our own children don't go to such fancy schools, so why
            should you?

UNCLE: Kwasi will go to Monkey Bay with your Uncle Mloza. You
            girls will come with me to Lilongwe. You will help with the
            household chores.

AUNT: And make yourselves useful!

JUNIE: We are grateful for your kind plan but we still would prefer
            to stay together. My fiancé, Noel, would certainly agree to
            marry me sooner than we had planned if I ask him to.
            Kwasi and Binti will live with us. We'll manage.

UNCLE: Ah, yes, Noel. His brother delivered this to you earlier.

JUNIE: You've read it? It is addressed to me.

UNCLE: What concerns you concerns us.

JUNIE: Dear Junie: I am writing to break off our engagement. My
            parents do not want me to marry into a family that has been
            tainted with AIDS, and I must respect their wishes. Noel.

JUNIE exits, crying.

BINTI: What about my radio show? I have to be on the radio.

UNCLE: Yes, it's too bad about that. That is money we will have to say goodbye to. You tape the show on Saturdays, yes?

BINTI: Yes.

UNCLE: I'll let you record one more show, then they will have to get somebody else. I have my own business to attend to.

I cannot stay in Blantyre any longer than that. Kwasi, be up early in the morning. You will go to Monkey Bay tomorrow.

BINTI: So, that was that.

Music. The three siblings embrace before separating.

Scene 8 — Lilongwe

BINTI: In Lilongwe, Aunt Agnes took everything from Junie and me. She even took my *Youth Times* newspaper with my interview in it. I got to keep my *Gogo's Family* script only because she didn't think it could be sold for anything. All we had to wear was our school uniforms and our night dresses. Everything else she kept for her own children or they sold. Junie was too sad to do anything about it. Whenever I tried to stand up for us, I would get punished. There was only one time that I felt special in Lilongwe. *(BINTI begins sweeping) Gogo's Family* came on the radio in Uncle Wysom's bottle shop where Junie and I worked. Uncle Wysom pointed me out to everyone and said:

UNCLE: My niece is the girl who plays Kettie on the radio.

BINTI: One of the customers asked me to sit next to him. He ordered me a Malawi shandy. He was telling me what was in it. Ginger ale, juice and—

JUNIE: *(pulling at her)* Get off that stool! *(to customer)* My sister is too young to sit in a bar.

BINTI: I wasn't doing anything wrong!

JUNIE: You stay away from the customers. When you go into the bar, you keep your head down, you gather up the empty bottles, and you get out of there.

BINTI: I was only —

JUNIE: I don't care. You listen to what I say. If you disobey me in this, you will be in such trouble!

BINTI: Junie was back to her old self again. And I was back to being treated badly by my uncle and his family. Especially my cousin Mary.

MARY enters.

MARY: You're too close to me. Move farther away.

BINTI: You can't tell me what to do.

MARY: I can so. You're just an orphan. You're nothing. You have to do what I say.

BINTI: I'm older and I don't have to listen to you.

MARY: Get away from me! Your mother died of AIDS!

BINTI: She did not.

MARY: She did, too. And your father.

BINTI: My mother and father were good people. They didn't go around spreading lies like some people's parents.

MARY: Your parents died of AIDS, and you probably have AIDS, too. Mama says I'm to stay away from you, or you'll give it to me.

BINTI: Oh yeah? How far away from me do you think you'll have to stay to be safe from AIDS?

MARY: Well, at least this far away.

BINTI: So if I come a little bit closer, will you be in danger?

MARY: You better stay back.

BINTI: What if I come this close? You need to be specific.

MARY: Stay away from me.

BINTI: And I suppose if I touch you on the arm, you'd catch AIDS for sure.

MARY: Don't touch me! Mama says you're not supposed to touch me! Mama!

BINTI: Is this how I'm not supposed to touch you?

BINTI touches MARY.

MARY: Mama! She's touching me!

BINTI: Or how about this? Or this?

Then Aunt Agnes came in and raised her hand to strike me. (*BINTI anticipates the blow*) I prepared myself for it. But her hand remained in the air.

Aunt Agnes was afraid to hit me because she thought she would catch AIDS.

So, she used a fly swatter instead of her hand.

BINTI reacts to the blows.

MARY exits.

JUNIE enters. She tends to BINTI's wounds.

JUNIE: Can't you just keep quiet?

BINTI: I was teaching Mary a lesson.

JUNIE: You weren't teaching her anything. You were just making things worse.

Scene 9 — Lilongwe and Mulanje

BINTI: We couldn't wait to get away from Uncle Wysom's family. Junie and I made a plan to get out of Lilongwe. We'd been saving my radio money and the money that Junie got from being nice to men in the bottle shop. But Mary had to ruin everything.

MARY enters.

MARY: Papa! Look at all the money that I found! It was in the storage room where they sleep.

UNCLE enters.

UNCLE & MARY: Thief!

BINTI: No. It's our money!

UNCLE: I will not turn you out on the street for stealing from me. I will also not turn you over to the police, although I should. You can stay with us for another few days while we find another place for you to go. Some family who needs workers.

Please stay out of our way until then.

UNCLE exits.

BINTI: When I woke up the next morning, Junie was gone. She left me a note telling me to find my way to Gogo's house in Mulanje.

JUNIE: We'll all be together again, I promise.

BINTI: I sneaked into the bottle shop and broke open the cash box for bus fare. The depot was crowded and so was the bus. But soon I fell asleep.

DRIVER: Last stop.

BINTI: I stepped off the bus. *(she gasps)* During the ride, Mount Mulanje rose above the town, rocky and glorious, with patches of mist stuck here and there for decoration. It sat in a cushion of deep green slopes and rose up all of a sudden as if it had been wandering and just decided that this would be a good place to stay.

Then, I went to the first church I saw. I knew what I had to do.

Music transition.

Scene 10 — Mulanje

Music.

BINTI: I walked up to the front of the church just like Gogo did at Bambo's funeral.

(to CONGREGATION) I am looking for my grandmother. I came here to live with her, but she doesn't know it yet. Her name is Precious Phiri. She lives somewhere in Mulanje.

PASTOR: Does anyone know Precious Phiri?

JEREMIAH: I do!

BINTI: Jeremiah, the young man who went to Bambo's funeral with Gogo, stood up.

JEREMIAH: She's only four miles away and I would be happy to take her.

You have an older sister, don't you? Is she with you?

BINTI: No.

JEREMIAH: Her name is Junie, isn't it?

BINTI: Yes.

JEREMIAH: Is she well?

BINTI: Yes, her name is Junie. And no, I don't think she's well, but I don't know for sure because I don't know where she is. Junie's boyfriend called off the engagement and our uncle treated us very badly. It's all our grandmother's fault.

JEREMIAH: Calm down, Binti.

BINTI: Why did she had to tell everyone that lie?

JEREMIAH: It wasn't a lie. The truth can hurt sometimes, but lies hurt even more. I don't know what happened with your uncle, but I can imagine. You're here now, and you are most welcome. I'll take you to your grandmother, and you can tell her yourself what happened. I'll do my best to find your sister. My bicycle is this way.

JEREMIAH sits as if on a bicycle.

Here, sit on my supply box.

They begin to ride. BINTI and JEREMIAH yell to be heard.

BINTI: What supplies do you have?

JEREMIAH: Condoms, brochures about HIV, blood-testing kits. I'm a peer counselor and I travel on my bike to talk to other young people — well, any people, actually — about protecting against AIDS, and how to take care of themselves if they have AIDS.

BINTI: I thought people just died if they had AIDS.

JEREMIAH: It's true that there is no cure. People in rich countries have AIDS drugs that help a lot, but few people here can afford them. But that doesn't mean we are helpless.

BINTI: Why did you say "we"?

JEREMIAH: I am HIV-positive.

              Hang on tighter. I'm a good driver, but we're going on some very bumpy trails.

BINTI: At first, I was nervous about putting my arms around Jeremiah. But he felt as normal as anybody. So I held on tight, forgetting about the HIV, and enjoyed my first bicycle ride.

              They ride for a short while in silence.

JEREMIAH: So, Junie's not engaged anymore?

BINTI: No. Jeremiah, will Gogo have room for me?

JEREMIAH: She always has room. Your grandmother is an important woman. She has a lot of power in this area and really holds the community together. You'll see.

BINTI: I thought that since my grandmother was so important and powerful, she probably had a nice house and people to help her clean it. Maybe I'd even get my own room. Maybe Gogo is even important enough to get me back on the radio.

JEREMIAH: Here we are.

              They dismount.

              Music transition and the sound of CHILDREN.

Scene 11 — Gogo's House

BINTI: I took a good look at a very small house with all the little children running around. *(to* JEREMIAH*)* There must be some mistake…

JEREMIAH: Your grandmother may be off visiting someone. Don't worry, she'll be back soon.

JEREMIAH exits.

BINTI: Jeremiah had said that Gogo was an important woman. Where was her important house?

GOGO enters.

GOGO: It's Binti! It's my granddaughter. Children, this is your cousin Binti.

BINTI: I wondered who all those children were… Two toddlers behind Gogo's skirt, two babies lying on a mat—

BINTI moves through the audience.

BINTI: Hello. Hi there. Nice to meet you. Hello. Ow, that's my foot. Hi. Hello. Hi. Hi. Hi.

There was a girl my age with another baby strapped to her back. Gogo said her name was Memory.

MEMORY: You can start by helping with supper. Maybe there's things in that bundle we can use too!

BINTI: You're not stealing my things, not you too! I don't have anything, I just have one blanket and one nightdress.

MEMORY: What's that?

BINTI: That's my script, it's all I have left. You're not taking it.

GOGO: Don't get upset. We're not taking anything from you, Binti. These things are yours and you do what you want with them. I'm sorry I trusted Agnes to look after you. All my good children died young. Come sit with me and tell me how you're doing, tell me about your brother and sister.

BINTI: I told her everything. I meant to skip over a few things — like stealing the money but it all came out.

GOGO: Give the rest of Wysom's money to Memory. We'll put it to good use. Don't worry.

MEMORY takes the money.

BINTI: Soon it was time to get ready for dinner. In the outhouse, I was sure that any minute spiders or snakes or even hippos would pop out. I had to wash my hands by pouring water on them with a scoop that was floating in a bucket. There were thirteen people for dinner and only three plates. I shared a plate of nsima *[pr. EN-simma]* with four of the small children. Everyone ate with their fingers! After dinner, we sat beside the fire. It was dark everywhere around me.

MEMORY: The mats are rolled out! Time for bed.

> *Kwasi and Junie lie on the ground.*

BINTI: Where do I sleep?

MEMORY: How about outside?

GOGO: Binti will soon get used to our ways.

> *Gogo lies down on the floor with the baby.*

MEMORY: Choose a spot. Quickly, the candle has to last.

> *Binti takes her blanket out of her bundle and lies down.*

MACHOZI: Can I share your blanket?

> *Machozi grabs a corner of her blanket and tugs it.*

BINTI: Hey!

GOGO: Lie down and go to sleep, Binti. The morning will be here soon. Shhh.

"In the olden days, very long ago, there were no stars in the sky
It was a girl child who put the stars there."

> *Binti ignores Machozi and wraps the blanket tightly around herself.*

GOGO: "She was on a long journey, and the night was very dark. She built a small fire, then threw the sparks from the fire high into the sky."

> *Machozi tugs on the blanket. Binti tugs back.*

GOGO: "They lit up a road for her in the darkness."

> *Machozi does one last tug, leaving Binti completely uncovered. Binti sits up, amazed.*

GOGO:	"And that is how we got to have stars."

MEMORY blows out the candle.

GOGO:	Good night, children.
ENSEMBLE:	Good night, Gogo.

BINTI lies down without her blanket and shivers.

Scene 12 — Gogo's House/The Pump

Rooster crows.

MEMORY:	Get some water. Hurry up.
BINTI:	You can't order me around. We're the same age.
MEMORY:	Well, start acting like it. We need water.
BINTI:	Let me wake up first.
MEMORY:	You look awake enough to me.
BINTI:	Where do I go?
MEMORY:	Machozi will show you where the pump is.
MACHOZI:	Follow me.

MACHOZI skips. BINTI tries to keep up.

BINTI:	How far is it?
MACHOZI:	Not far.
BINTI:	Wait for me.
MACHOZI:	We used to get water from a pond that made everybody sick, but some people from Canada built us a pump.
BINTI:	That's good.
MACHOZI:	Do you know where Canada is?
BINTI:	I'm not sure.
MACHOZI:	Is Canada in Malawi?
BINTI:	I don't think so.
MACHOZI:	Where are you from?

BINTI: Blantyre.

MACHOZI: Are you a real cousin or a pretend cousin?

BINTI: What are pretend cousins?

MACHOZI: Pretend cousins are…pretend cousins. Hurry before the line gets too long. Here we are!

BINTI: I've never done this before.

MACHOZI: Just watch how the women do it. Bye!

> *MACHOZI runs off.*

BINTI: Machozi, wait! I don't know where I am!

WOMAN 1: Where do you think you are? Where do you want to be?

> *WOMEN laugh. BINTI is too embarrassed to answer.*

WOMAN 2: Don't mind us. This is just our way of being friendly.

> *WOMEN pump water.*

BINTI: I watched the women work the pump so that I would know how to do it when my time came. One by one, the women lifted their pails and tubs of water onto their heads and walked off down the trails.

> *WOMEN walk with mimed water buckets. BINTI concentrates on pumping. WOMEN exit. BINTI lifts the heavy pail. She tries to put it on her head. It's too difficult so she carries it in her hands while walking*

BINTI: I headed down the trail that led back to Gogo's. *(she stops)* But nothing looked familiar. I was lost!

> *BINTI stands, holding the heavy pail, and starts to cry. MEMORY enters.*

MEMORY: Why don't you put the pail on your head?

BINTI: *(pulling herself together)* That's the old-fashioned way.

MEMORY: Oh, and it's the new, modern way to carry a pail of water in your hands so that your shoulders get sore and half the water spills onto the path.

BINTI: I'm so hungry. Why is there no food?

MEMORY: We'll eat tomorrow after school. First we go to school, then we go to the feeding centre.

BINTI: But why is there no food at Gogo's house?

MEMORY: Because your father died.

MEMORY exits.

BINTI: *These* were the "cousins" Bambo sent all that money to.

Scene 13 — Gogo's House/School/Orphan Club

Music.

MEMORY: That night, Binti asked Gogo if I was a pretend cousin or a real cousin.

GOGO: There are NO pretend cousins! You are all my grandchildren, and you are all real cousins. Do you understand?

BINTI: Yes, Grandmother.

I thought about asking Machozi which cousins were real and which were pretend but she would probably tell Gogo and Gogo would be furious. After all, it didn't matter if Memory was a real or pretend cousin. I was stuck with her.

The next day, we went to school.

Lights shift. ENSEMBLE become children at school.

MEMORY: You were so worried about how dirty and ragged your school uniform was.

BINTI: But when I got to the school, everyone else wore regular clothes. School was very different here. Instead of having textbooks and notebooks, we had to memorize things and repeat them back to the teacher. I was good at Reading but it was really hard doing Math that way. Afterwards, Memory led the way.

MEMORY: Get the others. Make sure we leave no one behind.

BINTI: I hope we don't have to do Math again tomorrow.

JUNIE and KWASI play a game.

MEMORY: We won't be going to school tomorrow. It's only two days a week.

BINTI: Two days a week? That isn't much.

MEMORY: We used to have it every day, but our teachers kept dying. For nearly a year we didn't have any school. The teacher we have now travels around between schools.

BINTI: Where are we going now?

MEMORY: To the Orphan Club. We always go there after school. Hurry up so we can eat.

              KWASI and JUNIE run to keep up.

BINTI: I ran to keep up with Memory and the others. When we got there, there were so many children. *(to MEMORY)* Are all these children orphans?

MEMORY: Did you think you were the only one? Go help the women cook.

BINTI: Cook? Me? An old woman shoved a wooden spoon into my hand so I began to stir a pot of nsima.

OLD WOMAN: Not like that. Put your body into it! Stir from the shoulder or it will burn and the food will be ruined.

BINTI: Like this?

OLD WOMAN: This girl's never cooked in her life.

              OLD WOMAN takes away spoon and stirs.

BINTI: I helped Memory put mats down for the meal instead. One of the women led the children in a song. Then there was a prayer. Finally, it was time to eat.

              I got a plate to myself. The food was delicious in my mouth and felt wonderful in my stomach. All of us washed our own plates, even the small kids. Then it was time for more singing and a play.

              BOY enters.

BOY: Can we borrow your blazer?

BINTI: It's mine.

BOY: We'll give it back to you. We're not thieves. We just want to use it for our play.

BINTI: Can I be in it?

BOY: All the good parts are taken, but you can be one of the sisters.

BINTI: Where's the script?

BOY: What do you mean?

BINTI: The story—

BOY: There's no time to tell you the whole story. You're one of the sisters.

GIRL: Just do what we do.

BINTI: I stuck close with the girls who played my sisters.

BOY: The play was about a mean uncle who took in his brother's children when they were orphaned.

BINTI: The boy wearing my blazer played him. So much of what happened in that play was like what had happened to Junie and me when we left Blantyre. I hated that I didn't know what was going on and what I was supposed to do.

MEMORY: The play had a happy ending.

BOY: The uncle died of AIDS.

GIRL: And the children had a party in the house that now belonged to them.

> CHILDREN *and* BOY *cheer and bow.* BINTI *bows a moment behind.* CHILDREN *exit.*

BOY: You haven't acted before, have you?

BINTI: I certainly have, but I've always had a script.

BOY: What's a script?

BINTI: It's paper with the words of the play printed on it.

BOY: Anybody can act if they're given the words. But don't worry. You'll do better next time.

BINTI: For the rest of the night, I kept thinking about the boy's words and remembered how awkward I felt during the play and how comfortable all the other kids were. If anybody could act with a script, why was I chosen for the radio show? I had a lot to learn.

> *BINTI lies on the floor and covers herself with her blanket.*

COUSINS: Goodnight, Gogo. Good night, Binti. Good night. Night.

BINTI: Good night.

> *MEMORY blows out the candle*

Scene 14 — Gogo's House

> *Rooster crows.*

> *MEMORY enters. She is holding a baby.*

MEMORY: Sometimes there were four babies. Sometimes only one. Some days, one toddler left…and was soon replaced with another.

> *BINTI enters.*

BINTI: *(to MEMORY)* Why are there always so many children?

MEMORY: Gogo looks after them when their own mothers are too sick to care for them.

BINTI: *(checking that the coast is clear)* So, they're not all real cousins, then.

MEMORY: Aren't these children good enough to be your real cousins?

BINTI: Don't be so touchy. *(indicating baby MEMORY holds)* When does he go back to his mother?

MEMORY: The baby is a she. You don't even know that. You don't even know her name, Binti.

> *MEMORY sits. It is clear now that she is breastfeeding.*

BINTI: How can you do that? I mean, I thought you had to be a mother before you could…

MEMORY: This is my daughter.

BINTI: But you're my age.

MEMORY: Gogo said I should tell you. She said you needed to know, but I don't care if you know or not.

I went to live with an uncle just like you did. My uncle's friend had AIDS. I had never gone with anyone before so he thought he would be cured by making me go with him.

BINTI: Go with him where?

MEMORY: He made me go with him as if I was his wife.

BINTI: Oh.

MEMORY: He didn't get cured. He still has the AIDS. He gave it to me, and he gave me this baby. When I came here, I wanted to forget everything, but Gogo wouldn't let me. She said I should change my name to Memory, so that every day I remember will be a curse to that man. She says the curse will be stronger if I live and be well.

BINTI: I couldn't imagine having a baby.

MEMORY: Here.

BINTI: But I've never held a baby.

MEMORY: It's all right.

BINTI takes the baby from MEMORY.

BINTI: She looks just like you. *(to audience)* I had so many questions but only one of them seemed to need an answer right away.

(to MEMORY) What's her name?

MEMORY: Her name is Beauty.

BINTI: There are no pretend cousins.

Scene 15 — Gogo's House

RADIO ANNOUNCER: *(v/o)* And now, it's time for *Gogo's Family.*

CHILDREN: We have a surprise for you, Binti.

MEMORY: One of Gogo's neighbours let her borrow his radio.

BINTI: I listened with the others, remembering my times in the studio, remembering how it felt to be so special, how much I'd loved hearing Mr. Wajiru say, over and over, "Talk like real people!"

GOGO: That's my Binti, on the radio.

BINTI: Everyone applauded. They wanted to know how I could be on the radio and sitting with them in Mulanje at the same time.

ENSEMBLE: Tell us the story of being on the radio.

BINTI: I felt shy at first but it was fun doing impressions of the director telling the cast: "You need to do it again!" People called me…

ENSEMBLE: "The Girl on the Radio."

BINTI: After the next week's episode, they asked me to tell the story again. I made it a little different. I pretended that I was trying hard not to sneeze during the taping. Even Memory laughed. I wondered what it must be like to be them, listening to my stories.

Most of the people had never been further than Mulanje.

MEMORY: Some had never left the village.

BINTI: I felt like the old Binti. But that feeling didn't last.

MEMORY: One week, another girl's voice came out of the radio. Another girl was playing the part of Kettie.

BINTI: They replaced me when I had to move.

GOGO: Never mind. We're much happier to have you here than far away on the radio.

BINTI: (*to audience*) I thought: There's nothing left. There's nothing left of me now…

MEMORY: Bit by bit, the strangeness of living with the cousins began to wear off for Binti.

> *BINTI goes about sadly doing her chores.*

Music. BINTI *pumps water. It gets easier and easier. She tries to balance the pail on her head. This gets easier too. She stirs a pot. It also becomes easier.*

GOGO: I'm so proud of you, Binti. Look how far you've come.

BINTI: Thank you, Gogo. *(to audience)* I was busy all day which was good because I'd go to sleep easier when I was tired. But I missed my old life and every day I thought of Kwasi and you and your promise:

JUNIE: We'll all be together again.

BINTI & JUNIE: I promise.

Scene 16 — Gogo's House

GOGO: I am done! I am done with my children! The ones who made me proud are dead. The ones who are left are not fit to be children of mine!

BINTI: Jeremiah brought news about Kwasi.

KWASI: Uncle Mloza sent me to jail for stealing food.

BINTI: Our brother had been treated as badly as me and Junie had been.

MEMORY: Gogo went from house to house, looking for bits of money that would help her get to Monkey Bay to free Kwasi.

BINTI: The people who could help, did. She and a neighbour woman left the next day.

GOGO: Take care of the little ones. I'll be back soon.

BINTI: Good-bye, Gogo.

   GOGO exits.

MEMORY: She shouldn't be going.

BINTI: Why not? Gogo's just doing what's good for the family.

MEMORY: What about what's good for her? Did you know she's sick?

BINTI: Gogo is sick?

MEMORY: She worries a lot. It's not good for her. Is your brother going to make more or less work?

BINTI: What do you mean?

MEMORY: Will he help out, or will he want to be looked after?

BINTI: No worries about Kwasi. You'll see.

MEMORY: Oh yes? You've been moping around here as though you were the only one who's lost something.

BINTI: I do my share of the work.

MEMORY: Yes, you work, but you still don't act like you're one of us. Not really. You act like you've been stuck here by accident and you're waiting for someone to fish you out. Like you're special.

BINTI: Well, I was special! Once.

MEMORY: Oh, yes, the radio. That will be what you tell people all your life, "I was once on the radio."

BINTI: What do you know about it? You don't know what it's like to have something so wonderful, and then to lose it.

MEMORY: Really, Binti, sometimes you don't make any sense.

         MEMORY exits.

Scene 17 — Gogo's House

BINTI: The next morning I woke up with a dull pain in my belly and a throbbing in my head.

         She looks down; really awake now.

         Blood? I've got the AIDS! I've got the AIDS!

         MEMORY enters.

MEMORY: Didn't your mother ever tell you about the monthlies?

BINTI: *(realizing, calming down)* My sister did.

MEMORY: I'll get you my cloths.

BINTI: Don't you need them?

MEMORY: I don't have the monthlies as long as I'm feeding Beauty. These cloths were my mother's dress.

BINTI: Thank you. Here.

BINTI takes off her pin and hands it to MEMORY.

MEMORY: For me?

BINTI: This is my prefect pin.

MEMORY: What's a prefect?

BINTI: One step away from Head Girl.

MEMORY: That must have been special.

BINTI: It was.

Scene 18 — Gogo's House

Music: "Ngewindzi." ENSEMBLE sings and dances together.

BINTI: Gogo convinced Uncle Mloza to drop the charges. We all waited for them to return from Monkey Bay. Finally, after six days…

KWASI: Binti!

KWASI enters and the two run into each other's arms.

BINTI: Kwasi! You're taller!

Music. Celebration as BINTI and her brother are reunited.

BINTI: It was like one of those miracles the pastor was always saying would happen but that I had never seen.

KWASI: It is so good to be here.

BINTI lets KWASI out of the hug and they sit.

BINTI: I hope Jeremiah finds Junie soon.

KWASI: He will. He's in love with her.

BINTI: But he has AIDS.

KWASI: So? AIDS affects the blood, not the heart.

            *Kwasi sees MEMORY. There is a connection. BINTI
            doesn't notice.*

BINTI: There wasn't much more talking that night. Gogo was
            tired and Kwasi was overwhelmed.

MEMORY: You'll have to fit into our little house.

KWASI: It's still less crowded than prison.

BINTI: And there's not much food.

KWASI: There's more than I had at Uncle Mloza's house. I didn't
            mind all the work but I couldn't get used to being so
            hungry. The family had food but they wouldn't share it
            with me. There's more here than at prison too. And here I
            don't have to fight anyone for it.

BINTI: He got along with everyone.

            *KWASI and MEMORY share a look which BINTI doesn't
            notice.*

BINTI: Kwasi was so much help at Gogo's house. I introduced him
            to all the cousins. All the little ones loved him.

            BINTI sees another look between KWASI and MEMORY.

BINTI: Oh, for heaven's sake. Am I the only normal person
            here?

            *BINTI exits. KWASI sneaks another look at MEMORY
            before he too exits.*

Scene 19 — Gogo's House

            *A BABY cries and cries. It grows weaker and then
            stops.*

BINTI: A few weeks later, one of the baby cousins was gone.

MEMORY: His own mother had died just the week before.

GOGO: Children can die of broken hearts just like adults. He was
            too sad to fight his sickness.

KWASI: We can build a coffin.

BINTI: We have no lumber or tools.

KWASI: He's not too heavy. We can weave together reeds and sticks.

JUNIE exits to upstage.

BINTI: I borrowed a machete to make notches in the bigger sticks and joined them together the way Bambo had showed me. Then we tied reeds around the joints to make them tighter. It worked.

MEMORY: Kwasi used a burnt stick to draw a bird inside the little child's coffin.

KWASI: "Tears go into our coffins. Tears make the coffins lighter and make the dead rise faster to heaven. It is harder to get to heaven if no one cries for you."

BINTI: That's what Bambo used to say.

MEMORY: Two days later, a man came by.

BINTI: He asked if we had made the coffin for the little boy and if we could build another for his son. He wanted to bury him with dignity but he had no money.

MEMORY: Can you help us repair our roof?

BINTI: The man said that he would do his best. I would have done it for free. He looked so sad.

MEMORY: He'd still be sad and our roof would still have holes. You build the coffins. I'll talk to the customers.

BINTI: And that's how we got into the coffin business.

MEMORY: We should make a sign to let people know what we're doing — and we need a name…

KWASI: Heaven Shop Coffins. Our coffins will take you swiftly to heaven!

BINTI: Just like in Blantyre, it was a good business to be in. In the first few days, we made three more baby coffins. Memory took the orders. One neighbour paid in yams and another in cash.

MEMORY: Gogo, if we buy lumber and tools, we can use them to make more money.

BINTI: Or we can get an extra pail to cut down on trips to the pump.

GOGO: I have smart grandchildren. You'll decide.

BINTI: Memory and Kwasi went to town and came back with boards and tools.

Kwasi and Memory enter running.

KWASI: We even have money left over!

BINTI: Let's tell Gogo!

They rush to Gogo and look to the spot where she sleeps.

KWASI: Gogo, you should have heard how Memory bargained for the extra tools.

BINTI: Gogo? Gogo, wake up!

An awful realization comes to all of them.

MEMORY: She's gone. Our Gogo's gone.

Music.

Scene 20 — Funeral

Lights shift. Company sings.

BINTI: Our relatives didn't come to the funeral. Gogo had asked the pastor to tell them if anything happened to her to stay away. They had hurt us, and should not be given the chance to do it again.

PASTOR: This good woman did the work of ten people here on earth. The love she showed her children can be seen in this magnificent coffin they built for her so she can have a peaceful rest now that her work is done.

BINTI: He told everyone at the funeral to continue Gogo's work by coming to us for the coffins they need.

MEMORY: And they did.

BINTI: So me, Kwasi and Memory were running the new Heaven Shop Coffin business and taking care of ourselves and the little cousins. When we had extra, we shared it. That's how Gogo would have wanted it. Only one thing was missing.

BINTI & KWASI: One person, actually.

Music.

Scene 21 — Gogo's House

KWASI: Jeremiah found Junie!

JUNIE: I was living in Muloza right on the border with Mozambique.

BINTI: Only twenty miles away.

MEMORY: She's sharing a small house with several other women and they entertain truck drivers to earn money.

KWASI: You can't say things like that about our sister!

BINTI: Kwasi.

MEMORY: There is some more news, I'm afraid. The men pay more if they don't have to use a condom. Jeremiah says Junie is HIV-positive and she is ashamed to come here.

KWASI: He's a liar!

MEMORY: Calm down, Kwasi. Junie lost herself the same way I did when my uncle's friend used me.

BINTI: And I felt lost too when I was in Lilongwe.

MEMORY: Gogo helped us and we can help Junie.

KWASI stands, purposefully.

KWASI: Get yourself ready, Binti. We're going to get our sister.

KWASI and MEMORY hug as KWASI departs.

Scene 22 — Muloza/Gogo's House

KWASI: We walked down the highway and hitched a ride on the back of a tea truck with children who worked on tea plantations.

BINTI: We sat on sacks of leaves.

KWASI: In a very short time, we were in Muloza.

BINTI: I looked across the border at Mozambique.

KWASI: It looked the same as Malawi.

BINTI: I couldn't wait to see Junie.

They climb out of the truck. They walk.

KWASI: The neighbourhood had small houses spread out behind the highway and bottle shops.

BINTI: One house looked as small and shabby as the others but the dirt yard had been freshly swept and there were some flowers growing along the side.

KWASI: This looks like Junie's place.

BINTI: The door opened just as Kwasi was about to knock and there was—

KWASI: Junie!

JUNIE: Kwasi!

KWASI and JUNIE embrace.

JUNIE: Binti!

JUNIE hugs BINTI.

BINTI: You just left me there!

JUNIE: I thought it was the best thing to do.

JUNIE tries to hug her. BINTI refuses and moves away from her.

BINTI: You could have taken me with you!

JUNIE: Don't cry, Binti.

JUNIE wipes away BINTI's tears as she continues to sob.

JUNIE:	Let me look at you. You're not a child anymore, are you?
	JUNIE hugs her again. BINTI begins to calm down.
BINTI:	Do you know about Gogo?
JUNIE:	Jeremiah told me.
KWASI:	Pack your things, we're going home.
BINTI:	And hurry up, "or you'll be in such trouble."
	Music.

Epilogue

BINTI:	When we got back to Mulanje, I was so excited to show you our new home. I hoped that you wouldn't think it was too shabby or that the new Heaven Shop Coffins was too rough.
JUNIE:	It's perfect. Bambo would be proud.
	MEMORY enters.
BINTI:	I crossed my fingers that the two bossiest people in the world would get along.
JUNIE:	You must be Memory. This chinjte cloth is for you.
MEMORY:	Thank you.
JUNIE:	Jeremiah told me so much about you. And this must be Beauty. (*she kisses the baby*) It's good that we're all together again.
BINTI:	She brought treats for everyone.
MEMORY:	The basin's perfect for giving the little ones their baths.
JUNIE:	Kwasi, this paper and coloured pencils are for you.
KWASI:	Thank you!
	He immediately sits and begins to sketch.
JUNIE:	And a book for you.
	JUNIE hands BINTI a book.

BINTI: *Plays for Young Actors*. Thank you.

JUNIE: You were so good in the radio show. You should keep practicing, and be an actor when you grow up. You can do plays for everyone. Here's one more thing for you.

        JUNIE hands the newspaper to BINTI.

BINTI: The *Youth Times* with my interview.

JUNIE: Someone was selling old newspapers in the street. I knew you'd like to have it again. It's something to be proud of, Binti.

        BINTI walks toward the audience and opens the paper, looking at the picture.

BINTI: Look at me standing in front of the microphone. Did I really march around town showing off my script? It's so embarrassing. But, Junie was right. I should be proud. I did a good job on the radio. But, now I have other things to be proud of too. I stood up to Aunt Agnes even though it meant a beating. I carry water, cook nsima and look after the small children who need me. And I have learned that there is sorrow in life but there's laughter too…and belonging and being needed and wanted.

MEMORY: *(calling out)* Binti, there is water to fetch and food to prepare!

BINTI: See?

        MEMORY and KWASI exit. JUNIE looks back at BINTI.

BINTI: First we eat, then we sleep and tomorrow, we will all make it through another day.

        She exits with JUNIE.

The End

Production History

Binti's Journey was commissioned with the support of Janice Wright and developed by Theatre Direct with the support of the Canada Council for the Arts' Supplementary Funds Initiative. The play premiered in February, 2008 at Tarragon Theatre Extra Space. Special thanks to workshop actors Matthew Brown, Audrey Dwyer and Junia Mason.

Director	ahdri zhina mandiela
Dramaturge	Lynda Hill
Set and Costume Design	Melanie McNeill
Lighting & Sound Design	Duncan Morgan
Movement & Music Director	Welcome Ngozi

Binti	Jajube Mandiela
Junie/Mr. Wajiru/Machozi/Gogo	Lisa Codrington
Kwasi/Jeremiah/Boy/Gogo	Sefton Jackson
Memory/Reporter/Mary/Gogo	Sodienye Waboso

Binti's Journey was remounted in February and March 2009, co-produced by Theatre Direct Canada and Manitoba Theatre for Young People with the following company:

Director	ahdri zhina mandiela
Dramaturge	Lynda Hill & Thomas Morgan Jones
Set and Costume Design	Melanie McNeill
Lighting & Sound Design	Duncan Morgan
Movement & Music Director	Welcome Ngozi

Binti:	Jajube Mandiela
Junie/Mr. Wajiru/Machozi/Gogo	Lisa Codrington
Kwasi/Jeremiah/Boy/Gogo	Patrick Amponsah
Memory/Reporter/Mary/Gogo	Sodienye Waboso

Following the run, this same company performed the show at the newly opened Wychwood Arts Barns in Toronto.

African songs were used to underscore and transition scenes. They were selected and taught to the company by Welcome Ngozi.

Please note that all publicity materials and programmes should indicate that *Binti's Journey* is adapted from the novel *The Heaven Shop* by Deborah Ellis.

About the Playwright

Marcia Johnson is the 2009/10 Ontario Arts Council Playwright-in-Residence at Roseneath Theatre. Her previous residency grant at Blyth Festival led to *Courting Johanna*, based on Alice Munro's short story "Hateship, Friendship, Courtship, Loveship, Marriage," which premiered at Blyth in 2008 and was published by Scirocco Drama. Also a librettist, Marcia wrote the short opera *My Mother's Ring*, which was nominated for a Dora Mavor Moore Award for Outstanding New Opera. Marcia began her career as an actor and still appears on stage and on TV and film. She appeared in *The Real McCoy* at Factory Theatre in Toronto and Great Canadian Theatre Company (Ottawa), *The Gladstone Variations* at the Toronto Fringe Festival and on CBC's *This is Wonderland*, CTV's *De Grassi: The Next Generation* and Global's *da kink in my hair* to name a few productions. Marcia is one of the featured Canadian playwrights at the 2009 International Women Playwrights Conference in Mumbai, where she will read from her play *Say Ginger Ale*.

Interview

When Lynda Hill, Theatre Direct's Artistic Director, offered me the commission to write a play for young audiences, I was thrilled. I had discovered my love of theatre while sitting on the gym floor of my Toronto public school during performances by touring theatre companies. It seemed like a great opportunity to pass on some of the same magic that I had experienced so long ago.

When I learned that the project was to adapt *The Heaven Shop* by Deborah Ellis, I felt honoured and humbled. *The Heaven Shop* is a beautiful and painful story about the effect of AIDS on children in Africa including discrimination and poverty. I admired how Ellis had created characters with whom the reader could empathize. She didn't pull punches about the realities of living under the shadow of AIDS. The book is very popular among middle school students. I knew that they would hold the play version to a very high standard. This would be a far cry from the dancing fairies and talking frogs from my days as a young audience member.

This was the first time that I had been approached by a theatre company to write a script based on an idea that wasn't self-generated. Also, I was asked to write in a style (narration or direct address) that I rarely used.

I presented an outline of what I wanted to write. It was no easy task deciding which characters and which scenes to include or cut. After Lynda's feedback, I created a second draft of the outline upon which both Lynda and director ahdri zhina mandiela agreed.

During the writing of the first draft, I was lucky enough to work with ahdri, Lynda, musician/composer Welcome Ngozi and two excellent actors. We lifted sections of the book for them to improvise around. Welcome chose African songs from his vast repertoire to pair with the scenes. There was a public reading of an excerpt from the developing play which was invaluable toward continuing with the writing.

A few months later came another workshop with a public reading of the full script for students that were the target age. The workshop and reading inspired more changes that were reflected in the script for the first production.

In that first draft, there was the odd acknowledgement to the audience but, for the most part, it was a naturalistic interpretation of the book. Binti was not as front and centre as she needed to be as the protagonist of the story. The young audiences needed their heroine to guide them through crucial, life-changing episodes of her life. I added more and more narration with each draft.

During the first run, I had the opportunity to watch the show with a student audience. Although the response was favourable, I felt that too much of the dialogue had been cut.

Fortunately, I got the opportunity to do rewrites for a second production. I feel that I was able to create a more satisfying balance between the naturalistic dialogue that I like to use and the storytelling that Theatre Direct is known for. Playwrights do not often have the opportunity of a second chance at a script once it's been produced, so I felt extremely lucky.

I believe that the play is quite flexible. It can be done with as many or as few cast members as a company decides.

The words are what matters. They began with the honest answers given to Deborah Ellis of real children in Malawi, her beautiful translation of them into the powerful book *The Heaven Shop*, and finally in my attempt to turn it all into a play for young people.

I'm glad that meaningful theatre is being created for children and teens. I hope that *Binti's Journey* will one day be a historical piece when people can recall AIDS and poverty in the past tense.